Contents

Acronyms and Abbreviations

ACC	Administrative Committee on Coordination
BPRM	Bureau for Planning and Resource Management (in UNDP)
CAP	Consolidated Appeal Process
CERF	Central Emergency Revolving Fund
CFA	Committee on Food Aid, Policies and Programmes
CCPOQ	Consultative Committee on Programme and Operational Questions
DAC	Development Assistance Committee
DHA	UN Department of Humanitarian Affairs
DMT	Disaster Management Team
DMTP	Disaster Management Training Programme
DPA	UN Department of Political Affairs
DPKO	UN Department of Peace-Keeping Operations
ECHO	European Community Humanitarian Office
ECOMOG	Economic Community Military Observer Group
ECOSOC	Economic and Social Council
ECOWAS	Economic Community of West African States
ERC	Emergency Relief Coordinator
ERD	Emergency Response Division
ERO	Emergency Relief Operations
EHA	Emergency and Humanitarian Action
FAC	Food Aid Convention
FAO	Food and Agriculture Organization of the United Nations
HBP	Health as a Bridge for Peace
Hedip	Health and Development for Displaced Populations
IASC	Inter-Agency Standing Committee
IBRD	International Bank for Reconstruction and Development
ICJ	International Court of Justice
ICRC	International Committee of the Red Cross
IDNDR	International Decade for Natural Disaster Reduction

IDP	internally displaced person
IEFR	International Emergency Food Reserve
IFI	International Financial Institution
IFOR	Implementation Force (Bosnia and Herzegovina)
IFRC	International Federation of Red Cross and Red Crescent Societies
IGO	Inter-governmental Organization
ILO	International Labour Organisation
IOM	International Organization for Migration
IPPNW	International Physicians for the Prevention of Nuclear War
IRIN	Integrated Regional Information Network (West and East Africa)
MSF	Médecins sans Frontières
MCDA	Military and Civil Defence Assets (UNDRO)
MCDU	Military–Civilian Disaster Unit (DHA)
MDM	Médecins du Monde
MoU	Memorandum of Understanding
NGO	Non-governmental Organization
OAS	Organization of American States
OCHA	Office for the Coordination of Humanitarian Affairs
ODA	Overseas Development Agency
OECD	Organization for Economic Cooperation and Development
OFDA	Office of Foreign Disaster Assistance (US)
OEOA	Office of Emergency Operations in Africa
OERC	Office of the Emergency Relief Coordinator
ONUCA	UN Observer Group in Central America
ONUSAL	UN Observer Mission in El Salvador
OOTW	Operations Other Than War
OSCE	Organization for Security and Cooperation in Europe
OSU	Operations Support Unit (UNDP)
OUNHAC	Office of the UN Humanitarian Assistance Coordinator
OUNS	United Nations System Support and Services

PAHO	Pan-American Health Organization
Res Rep	Resident Representative
SHD	Sustainable Human Development
SRSG	Special Representative of the Secretary-General
SURFs	sub-regional facilities
TRAC 3	Target for Resource Assignment from the Core
UNACC	UN Administrative Committee on Coordination
UNAMIR	UN Assistance Mission for Rwanda
UNAVEM II	UN Angola Verification Mission
UNDHA	UN Department of Humanitarian Affairs
UNDP	UN Development Programme
UNDRO	Office of the UN Disaster Relief Coordinator
UNERC	UN Emergency Relief Coordinator
UNESCO	UN Educational, Scientific and Cultural Organization
UNETF	UN Emergency Task Force
UNFPA	UN Fund for Population Activities
UNHAC	UN Humanitarian Assistance Coordination Unit
UNHCR	UN High Commissioner for Refugees
UNICEF	UN Children's Fund
UNITA	National Union for the Total Independence of Angola
UNOMIG	UN Observer Mission in Georgia
UNOSOM II	UN Operation in Somalia
UNOPS	UN Office for Project Services
UNITAF	Unified Task Force (Somalia)
UNPROFOR	UN Protection Force
UNRWA	UN Relief and Works Agency for Palestinian Refugees
UNTAC	UN Transitional Authority in Cambodia
UNTAES	UN Transitional Administration for Eastern Slavonia
UNTAG	UN Transition Assistance Group (Namibia)
WFP	World Food Programme
WHO	World Health Organization

Preface

The United Nations conducts a wide variety of operations through its specialized agencies, funds and programmes. Most of these organizations have long been poised – or more frequently, stretched – between long-term development and emergency response. This would almost certainly remain the case were their activities directed only at the relief of entrenched poverty and natural disasters. However, the number and variety of militarized humanitarian emergencies and the resurgence of United Nations peacekeeping has raised their profiles, challenged assumptions and further strained available resources and managerial resourcefulness. To this must be added the latest round of United Nations reform, which affects their capacities, relationships and calculation of priorities.

A number of the agencies' operational difficulties and dilemmas are a familiar component of the peacekeeping literature, at least in outline, but the extent of the present and predictable strains is striking within the context of contemporary peacekeeping and against the background of larger United Nations restructuring. This collection therefore focuses on those agencies which most often find themselves working within or beside UN-mandated peacekeeping operations. The 'UN agencies' of the title is a convenient shorthand for the variety of constitutional and organizational forms involved, much as the term 'peacekeeeping' is sometimes employed in a generic sense.

I would like to thank all of the contributors for the effort in producing these essays against the pull of their other, often considerable, commitments. In particular, I would like to thank Leon Gordenker and Thomas Weiss for their early support and generosity of spirit. I am grateful to the Editor of *International Peacekeeping*, Michael Pugh, for giving me the opportunity to undertake this edition. My colleagues in Cambridge – Jack Shepherd, Jane Brooks, Angela Pollentine and Kathleen Shepherd – provide friendship, support and the kind of working conditions one wouldn't sensibly hope for.

Jim Whitman

Clash and Harmony in Promoting Peace: Overview

LEON GORDENKER

The difficulties that beset the relationship between peace-maintenance and humanitarian assistance are not only an outcome of operational complexity, but can first be located in the disjuncture between relatively new organizational forms and dynamics outside or at odds with formal legal and political structures. Issues of authority, control, coordination and accountability have become more vexed as the growth and diffusion of humanitarian actors and processes clash with state-centric structures. The impacts on sovereign control, the roles of the UN agencies, the larger UN system and the prospects for its reform are considered, together with the prospects for institutional reforms and improvements to operational efficiency.

Blending international peace-maintenance and humanitarian relief invokes two opposed lines of doctrine and governmental practice.[1] The clash and harmony of the two lines took on special importance only in the last quarter of the twentieth century as governments and international organizations encountered a political and social environment that erupted with new challenges.

The nineteenth-century origin of international humanitarian institutions in the Red Cross movement still underlies the conventional doctrine of organizations offering aid to victims of war. That doctrine now broadly holds that all who are injured by the violence of conflict deserve succour. As for maintaining peace, serious institutions dedicated to it are as recent in origin as the First World War and the League of Nations. The League's successor, the United Nations, and a few other intergovernmental agencies have placed soldiers in the field to watch over armistice agreements and in rare instances to use force to end fighting. As armed strife diminishes or momentarily pauses, the accompanying human suffering becomes visible. Then the purveyors of humanitarian assistance offer help.

During the years since the Second World War, organized humanitarian assistance to victims of military action has reached many millions of people. It has saved countless lives. It is omnipresent in the man-made human

Leon Gordenker is Professor Emeritus of Politics and Research Associate of the Center of International Studies at Princeton University.

disasters that usually accompany military operations and bear the deceptively benign title of complex emergencies. These have stimulated still-novel forms of organization that have anything but settled into a final definition.

Concepts and Actuality

The contemporary conceptual design for the organized maintenance of peace fits only partly with actuality. To begin with, it is designed for international wars, but the UN system and regional international arrangements are increasingly engaged in intrastate conflicts – that is, civil wars, the deterioration of governments, liberation movements operating from outside territories, civil chaos resulting from misgovernment and failure to deal with natural disasters. Such conflicts take only a few days to dump thousands of needy displaced persons in perilous havens or outside their home states. The question of who is in charge of the territory and of the humanitarian assistance looms large and often without a convincing answer.

The speed with which a humanitarian disaster can develop owes much to modern technology. The fire power of hand-held weapons has been increasing exponentially while their cost declines markedly. As a result, a few armed men can wreak disaster, setting masses of people on the run while murdering others. A relatively small armed group can destroy the authority of an already feeble government. Their handiwork easily turns into the global news story of the day for media that observe few boundaries. The telephone and the Internet bring further poignant details to light. The stately pace of traditional diplomacy has little chance to rely on patience when demands for quick responses mount from popular sources, governments and humanitarian organizations. Private suffering in some but not nearly all instances becomes public grief, and both intergovernmental and private agencies mount relief efforts while peace-maintainers take their stations within a few days.

Humanitarian and military entities engaged in peace-maintenance[2] soon encounter organizational and policy friction, not to say conflict, among themselves and with each other. As the chapters that follow make clear, this secondary by-product of peace-maintenance develops at every level of organization. It encompasses organized intergovernmental relationships in the UN system. It induces hesitation and self-examination in the offices of both intergovernmental and non-governmental tenderers of assistance to victims of violence. It confuses agencies that sponsor long-term economic and social development. It spurs on criticism of coordination and rhetoric about confusion, waste and corruption. At the directing level in the field, organizational representatives passionately debate who does what. And at the level of the recipients, sometimes those who come to help do so in ways that trip each other up and add more harm to misery. Without denying the moral validity of humanitarianism, those who pose issues of policy, coordination and specialization in complex emergencies also implicitly call attention to fundamental contradictions in international politics.[3]

A World of Sovereigns

The most fundamental of these discrepancies grows out of the concept of a world of sovereign states, whose governments make joint decisions only by mutual consent and alone control activities within their territories. Their joint agreements have established the organizations of the UN family, including those that proffer assistance in complex emergencies. They are governed ultimately by intergovernmental organs. Their financing comes mostly from governments. They depend largely on the administrative apparatuses of member governments to carry out the policies to which they agree. Threats to or breaches of the peace are handled by conventional diplomatic conciliation procedures, and in some rare cases by coercive intervention against the violators.

International organizations that concentrate on the pacific settlement of disputes, such as the regional organizations provided for in the UN system, either were not intended to use military means or when they were, as with the UN, never received the promised commitments from governments. Consequently, military alliances such as the North Atlantic Treaty Organization, and *ad hoc* command structures patched together by the UN Security Council, can come into action in serious threats or breaches of the peace. But this implies no continuum of policy and organization from the quarrel to fighting to pacification with accompanying humanitarian activity along the way.

As complex emergencies involve the ability of governments to control events within the territory of their states, humanitarian assistance inevitably calls up some measure of friction with national administrations and ultimately the issue of sovereignty itself. Who is in charge? Does anyone have to be? Must assistance-givers be invited in, do they need permission, who gives it and who inspects them for conformity to local rules? Should the programmes be assembled in a coherent whole or is that impossible, too costly or unnecessary? Where should decisions be taken – at the delivery level, at the provincial or national level or in some distant international headquarters? How does the national and local administration fit into these efforts? Who is answerable for successes and failures in saving lives and helping those in trouble?

A further actual violation of the pristine concept of an international system made up of sovereign states derives from the rapid growth in terms of numbers and scope of what the United Nations calls non-governmental organizations.[4] Originally a loose category defined by intergovernmental organizations for the sake of convenient procedures, some NGOs have grown to full-fledged international collaborators. They not only advocate policy, furnish salient knowledge and build public awareness of the humanitarian aspects of peace-maintenance, but some of them also accept contracts to bring services to the affected areas.[5]

If NGOs as advocates and knowledge-transmitters function as analogs of interest groups in governments, those with transnational reach and support that enter state territory along with peace-maintainers have another character. They do work – such as caring for the displaced, feeding the hungry and protecting public health – that government agencies usually take on even in times of heavy military conflict. They thus deal directly with the subjects of states and, in a growing number of instances, join in deciding on the policies shaping their operations.

With the possible exception of the International Committee of the Red Cross, these NGOs have no standing in international law. They have the character of contractors, rather than agents, of international organization. In many cases of usually small scope, they work entirely without the sanction of international organization and in some cases without even the knowledge of the nominal government. They usually bring with them substantial numbers of foreign personnel. They may simultaneously efficiently perform their appointed tasks and get in the way of peace-maintenance. They can claim sanctity as humanitarians and yet wittingly or not lend support to belligerents.

While formal international organizations with their formula of states members have specific arrangements, such as annual reporting and reviewing by expert bodies and debates to promote accountability in the execution of their policies, NGOs usually make little use of such devices. Their decisions emerge from committees of officials with overall policy under the supervision of a board of trustees composed of notables, experts and others who are co-opted or in some cases appointed by governments. Not all of them make detailed reports about their work, and in some instances supervision by the governments of their headquarters locations is barely even scanty. In the universe of NGOs, attempts at self-regulation and the mutual setting of standards have begun. Moreover, the international organizations and governments who offer them contracts for field operations make judgements on NGOs and normally have insight into their responsibility but can hardly hold them fully accountable.

Despite vague understanding of precisely who and what NGOs

operating beside peace-maintainers may be, they nevertheless constitute some link to the 'civic society' which is otherwise unrepresented in formal international organizations.[6] As a legal proposition, the civic society is subject to the governments of states and has no place in the policy process of international organizations. As a fact in contemporary society, individuals and organizations outside formal governmental agencies organize to meet social needs. They regulate their lives within and sometimes outside legal structures. Increasingly their contacts beyond national frontiers have grown in depth and breadth. In conflict situations, whatever effect the civic society has on the government, the contending militaries and the peace-maintainers and humanitarian organizations may become sharply attenuated. Moreover, the local humanitarian NGOs may be overshadowed by their transnational and foreign cousins.

Using the System

A persistent dream among some advocates of peace and of humanitarian service holds that 'politics' can and should be avoided.[7] Whatever the basis for such visions, in actuality both peace-maintenance and associated humanitarian ventures pose classical political questions at a time when uncertainty clouds both present and future. They require decisions as to what ends are sought, what instruments can be employed to those ends, what services are to be delivered, how this is to be done, who has responsibility for them, who pays for them and who employs scarce resources. Such questions must be answered both at the beginning of and during peace-maintenance ventures. They constitute the stuff of politics.

When the United Nations or other international organizations striving to maintain peace are engaged, the paramount method of coming to political decisions is by diplomatic means. That may be done bilaterally or in the UN framework within intergovernmental organs. Against a background of particularistic interests, it involves negotiation of agreements, preferably to settle disputes and, if necessary, to employ armed force against offenders. But diplomats – representatives of governments – do not usually organize or manage either peace-maintenance or humanitarian programmes. This is done in dedicated organizational settings where officials, who may or may not have been involved in the diplomatic process of setting overall goals and policies, manage the execution of the mandated mess. The closer officials of these organizations are to the ultimate consumers of their products, the more attenuated the connections between policy-making and operations. Field operatives of necessity adapt their presence to the surroundings, which in complex emergencies can be troubled, unclear and dangerous.

Military operations, moreover, fall under the command of officers of national forces who are detached for UN service either under the supervision of the UN Secretary-General or reporting through channels to the Security Council. Despite formal instructions to report only through channels specified by intergovernmental decisions, commanders of units contributed by cooperating governments obviously communicate directly with their national headquarters. They have been known to go so far as to ignore directives coming through international channels.

Such intergovernmental agencies as the World Food Programme, the UN Children's Fund, the UN High Commissioner for Refugees and the UN Development Programme that come under the legal authority of the United Nations, and the associated specialized agencies, such as the World Health Organization that have their own legal bases in international conventions, all maintain strong organizational identities. Their organizational experience and aims become an important factor in the development of policies and programmes in connection with peacekeeping. They do not represent tools that, like a hammer, can be picked up and put down at will. Their chiefs soon edge close to the diplomatic process of setting out overall UN policies for a particular peace-maintenance operation that requires humanitarian services.

In a similar manner, NGOs that could take up contracts with the intergovernmental agencies become part of the political process in complex emergencies. Some of them can treat this process with coolness or even disdain as they rely entirely on non-governmental funding and support. Others may be sensitive to donor government pressures but not to the degree that they take on any offered assignment. Moreover, in accepting a role they have opportunities to affect initial policies and, by feedback from operations, to initiate changes. All NGOs moreover must accommodate to the governmental authorities or whoever is in charge where they operate.

Human Rights

The contemporary international interest in protecting human rights, developed to a firm policy over the last 50 years by the United Nations and other international organizations, cuts directly across state-centred diplomatic approaches to peace-maintenance and the humanitarian doctrine of helping whoever is in need.[8] As humanitarian emergencies, especially those involving internal strife, often grow out of massive denials of human rights, corrective international action may imply ignoring the sanctity of the sovereign state. Concern for human rights plunges deep into what happens within the national jurisdiction whether on the part of government or some other grouping. Merely ending fighting under the supervision of passive peacekeeping, or by employing a more active form using active civil or military measures, may leave the causes of the violation in place. Actually protecting human rights could mean destroying the authority of a government or dissident group and setting up another in its place.

Humanitarian activities too could conceivably contribute to further violations of human rights. Material assistance could fall into the hands of only the repressive group, giving it advantages over those who do not receive it. Food and medicine from outside could be seized by repressive military units. Humanitarian assistance could be efficiently directed to its users through a repressive entity, bolstering its prestige and grip on events but not diminishing its offences. Refugee camps supported by humanitarian organizations could be controlled by those who have caused the human rights violations and could be used as a base for guerrilla action. But to refuse assistance on the grounds that the recipient causes human rights violations contradicts the general humanitarian notion of helping those in need and puts the assisting organization into the impossible position of deciding who favours and who interferes with human rights.

Potential for Unhappy Results

The entire process of maintaining peace and trying to cope with the humanitarian implications almost invites difficulties.[9] The diplomatic process of negotiating decisions through national representatives calls up sometimes strong, sometimes obscure references to national interest. As many governments are involved, the outcome can be vague and face-saving rather than effective guidance for execution of policies. Furthermore, the same national considerations may be invoked in intergovernmental organs throughout the UN system leading to further bargaining outcomes.

Acting according to their doctrines and imperatives, executing organizations add another bargaining element to the relationship of peace-maintenance and humanitarian assistance. Even when they take the initiative, enter the field on their own and finance themselves, they must establish some connection with the peace-maintainers. Or if they choose to try not to do so, they risk their own necks as well as possibly causing diversions that harm the local population. Relationships between humanitarian organizations and military units, much recent experience shows, involves differences over procedures, aims, modes of operation and authority.

None of this necessarily leads to good management structures or practices. To begin with, neither decisions about mounting peace-maintenance nor humanitarian operations are made with a view to exemplary management. They tend to have a hurried, improvised character and in any case patch together organizational capacities that have evolved in incongruent patterns. Nor does institutional learning by itself offer an all-purpose formula as each incident tends to differ in significant detail from the last.

A further source of unhappy results lies in the reliance of intergovernmental organization on national governments to carry out policies. Peace-maintenance ventures have their origin precisely in the failure to governments to live up to their commitments not to threaten or employ force in their relationships. Many situations of civil strife have their origin in violations of human rights. To expect such embattled or incompetent governments to receive humanitarian assistance and distribute it as intended may be to lean on a slender reed.

Yet trying to substitute intergovernmental organization personnel or NGOs as sources of food, medicine, housing, social services and protection of human rights almost surely will involve serious errors that no local person would make. In addition, without some central policy as at least a reference point if not for the controlling instructions, humanitarian organizations may work at cross purposes. In some instances, the numbers of NGOs sending personnel and supplies may give the impression of chaos and wild gestures. To bring this together involves the process of matching skills and getting the consent of participants that is usually lumped under the term 'coordination'. Only a few missteps in such arrangements can cause quarrels that are damaging to the purposes of the operation and those who should receive assistance.

System Reform: Sisyphus in Turtle Bay

Reforming the United Nations system in order to provide better responses to political needs, manage operations more efficiently and increase accountability is anything but a new notion. It has been attempted repeatedly with the result that it has merely served as prelude for a new round. The ball of suggestions and proposals slips over the backs of the reformers into the wordy mire of Turtle Bay.

This frustration is unavoidable so long as governments pretend that they have little responsibility for acting on what they approve in the General Assembly and the Security Council. They can do so because all participants accept and defend themselves as agents of sovereign states that accept only that to which they have agreed. If they do not, only a few and then very rarely can be compelled to comply.

Plans for reforming the UN system focus mainly on the structures and practices of international secretariats that are the permanent custodians of intergovernmental policy. These plans usually take as given the claims of governmental inviolability that are implied in the notion of sovereignty.

They avoid the inherent difficulties of a decision-making process where exceptions based on claims of national interest are easier to find than commitment. The committees, commissions and experts charged with reporting generally seek structural changes based either on no new assumptions about the locus of authority or on fundamentally revised decisional processes. Or another bureaucratic control device, such as the recent creation of an Inspector-General's office in the UN Secretariat, is designed to plaster over what already exists.[10]

Consequently, official plans for reforming the United Nations concentrate, as in Secretary-General Kofi Annan's most recent attempt,[11] on the reorganization of the UN Secretariat and on responses to demands especially from the United States and from some other developed countries for lower costs and some measures that supposedly improve efficiency. Reform plans from unofficial sources usually have a similar tone and content but hardly specify what assumptions and methodology underlie their examinations. In the background are not only American domestic politics but also the assiduously promoted image of the United Nations as a vast, sticky bureaucracy.

As the UN bureaucracy, including the specialized agencies, would hardly serve a large city, much of the effort in reorganization amounts to pruning a bush with tools meant for felling a forest. Doing so may well drive away the most devoted young officials who see little future in such penurious enterprises. At the same time, the governments continue to assign tasks – witness the explosion of peacekeeping at the end of the 1980s and beginning of the 1990s – to international organizations without increasing expenditures. This can be described as a self-fulfilling prophecy of failure.

Almost all reform plans as well as studies of humanitarian operations in peace-maintenance insist on the need for coherence and coordination, which they treat as lacking or primitive. Horrible examples abound of waste, duplication, confusion and interference with political aims. While stupidities in any enterprise beg for correction, retrospective blame can help in future only if it points to correctable faults. Obviously the past cannot be replayed and patched up. What goes on into the future is formal organization. Therefore, reforms deal with organizational structures first and only afterwards with process – that is, how and why they interact. This may well set the cart before the horse.

While the Secretary-General can modestly rearrange the structure of the UN Secretariat and reassign existing staff members, his reach soon is exhausted. Governmental eagles keep continual watch over what happens to their nationals and their presumed national interest. Removing or even moving personnel can cause major rows for the Secretary-General. He has moreover practically no influence over the financial contributions to either the United Nations or other agencies in its group. The governments decide whether to pay up what they have offered during the UN process to assess themselves. Increasingly, willingness to meet these obligations declines as the bills come in for peacekeeping and the associated humanitarian work. The United States government is at the moment the notorious offender but is not alone.

As real reorganization inevitably costs money, in the form of time spent on planning, payments to staff members whose long-term appointments are cut short, recruitment of replacements and the like, expenses have to rise. Reorganization furthermore implies the possibility that more, not fewer, staff members and supporting infrastructure may be needed for efficient functioning. Yet the very governments that most energetically press for reform have also tried and usually succeeded in imposing zero real growth budgets on the UN system during the last decade.

The UN Secretary-General moreover has no grip on the intergovernmental UN specialized agencies among which WHO, the International Labour Organization and the Food and Agriculture Organization and its now loosely associated World Food Programme are the most relevant to humanitarian activity. These have their own governmental membership and their own associations with relevant ministries in governments. The input of national governments to their programmes is usually guided by different policy considerations from what goes into the United Nations. Coordination via the UN Economic and Social Council and the bureaucracy-based Administrative Committee on Coordination have repeatedly fallen short of their announced goals.

As for the more closely associated agencies, including UNICEF, UNDP and UNHCR, they have almost as much actual autonomy as the specialized agencies. While the Secretary-General formally appoints their heads, he does so only on the basis of approval by major donor governments. Each of these organizations has its own intergovernmental organ for overall policy and supervision. Each is financed almost entirely outside the UN budget through voluntary contributions from governments and, in the case of UNICEF, from considerable support from the civic society.

If reform of this collection of agencies, put together at different times for different goals, is to succeed, a good deal more is needed than pressure and normative tracts directed to the UN Secretary-General and his staff. All he can do with his sister agencies is to try to persuade. If governments generally back this persuasion, it might be successful in changing some management and programmatic dimensions. But governments do not agree, except in the most general terms, about either of these dimensions and they not infrequently follow different lines in different agencies.

What governments have constructed in both constitutional forms and in practice over 50 years obstructs real reform of the system. In all the agencies, intergovernmental control mechanisms monitor what the appointed managers do and make final decisions on budget levels and programme directions. The opportunities for government representatives to impede reforms by using votes and influence in the control mechanisms reach astonishing numbers. These are, moreover, relatively small organizations compared to the larger governments or large multinational corporations. Yet they are burdened with countless watchdogs. The budget, financing and policy processes obviously reflect the doctrine that no sovereign should be controlled by another and emphatically not by an international organization.

In the end, then, if the UN system is to reformed along the lines of good management or something else, the governments that designed it with inherent limitations to protect themselves will have at least to acquiesce in changing it. It is beyond the present limit of credibility to expect them to approve substantial changes in the authority of international organizations or to expect them to abandon all of the internal, obscure control mechanisms that they now enjoy. Moreover, nationalism, which has not diminished through UN activity, limits what some governments can do in international cooperation. Other governments, such as the United States, cannot count on legislative and popular support for UN reforms that would cost more or that would restrict their range of unilateral political and military manoeuvre.

At the level where national government policy and international organization reform join – that is, in the councils and committees of the UN system – the diplomatic procedures that have built the present system are the only ones available to reform it. Whether the diplomats who represent governments have the skills to create good structures for efficient management is at least subject to doubt. Whether the continual search for national advantage and prestige will remain cannot for the moment be doubted.

At the end of the day, the signs remain discouraging for either structural reform that counts for much, or programmatic reform in the short term. They could be reversed, perhaps, but not quickly. Their significance could also be fudged by adroit diplomatic constructions which give an acceptable gloss to actual improvement, but at most this would be superficial and probably not cumulative. Unless the way that governments approach international organization radically changes, the reform campaigns in Turtle Bay will go some distance up the slope only to be pulled back by the force of the state system.

At the level of programmes of humanitarian assistance, inherent difficulties also abound. Senior officials of humanitarian organizations must either take the lead in developing programmes or strive alongside the always-few national representatives who have the insight and political space to do so. They convince the intergovernmental oversight organs to approve proposed programmes. In most cases these grow out of what has already been undertaken. As in all organizational settings, a conservative, ameliorative bias emerges that aims at maintaining organizational integrity and protecting the boundaries of activity.

Most of the UN system has for the last four decades emphasized economic and to a lesser extent social development. Built around financing through UNDP and, more distantly, the World Bank, the resulting programmes depend largely on governmental demands and cooperation. The projects put in place on the ground are almost always in themselves long-term or are applied for long-term results. Other programmes consist mainly of agreements among governments to follow policy lines approved by themselves in intergovernmental organs as global recommendations. Intergovernmental organizations offer help in installing and applying such policies.

Even UNHCR, which deals with the needs of persons in situations of need and suffering, never was intended as a large-scale relief organization that could respond in complex emergencies along with military forces. Yet it has been incrementally reshaped, first to deal with mass refugee movements and then increasingly to work in peace-maintenance ventures. Similar evolutions have taken place in the operations of WFP, which has shifted from mainly development to mainly humanitarian relief. UNICEF early on dropped 'emergency' from its title in favour of development but has lately become prominent in complex emergencies. The UN Secretariat has striven under pressures from governments and NGOs to put together coordinating devices, such as its Department of Humanitarian Affairs. As will be seen below, these arrangements have gone through repeated metamorphoses and have satisfied none of their clients. Their leaders must contend with the centrifugal tendencies built into both the structure and process of international organization. At the same time, it is by no means clear that UN Secretariat has overcome the difficulties of coordinating its own policy mechanisms for peace-maintenance with other aspects of its work, including human rights and humanitarian responses.

The injection of NGOs as at least sometime, partial participants in the definition of policies and more importantly in the execution of programmes of international organizations, adds another complication and opportunity in the coordination of humanitarian work. The very number and diverse character of NGO operations presents a basic difficulty for coordinators. So does their remaining incongruity with a system based on intergovernmental agreement. Yet NGOs offer opportunities for coordination because of their connection with the civic society, their proximity to the end users of international assistance, their information about events at ground level and their growing expertise. Adroit engagement of all of these facilities could help with laying a basis for coordination.

The present organizational tangle reflects organic growth which could hardly be preceded by much precise planning. Rather it blossoms out from needs, opportunities, successes and errors. It could not be simplified effectively by any handy formula, such as a hierarchical command structure of a military model. Even if an attempt – practically inconceivable among sovereignty-based organizations – were made to build such a hierarchy, it would probably fall apart in encountering the clashing aims of those who respond to complex emergencies.

Two Cheers for More Muddling Through

International responses to expanded peace maintenance, in which international organizations patch together both military elements and humanitarian relief, have a considerable history of muddling through. Despite organizational difficulties and fumbling, in each assignment peace-maintainers have learned more about their new trade. Humanitarian organizations have a longer history and have operated in countless instances, usually without peace-maintainers in the neighbourhood. Where they have met, both elements have more often than not delivered impressive products, especially as compared with what could have been expected without the establishment of the UN system. If they have not achieved some theoretical optimum mode or organization, or if their functions do not quite mesh and they leave bitterness behind, they can hardly take the blame for the situations that require their presence.

The underlying question for peace-maintainers and humanitarian cooperators asks whether they could carry out their assigned tasks more efficiently and with less friction. No doubt they could. But this involves not merely organizational devices resting on the foundations of the state system as it was understood when the Second World War ended, but also adjustments in the exercise of state authority to take into account technological and social change. It is hardly an exaggeration to say that in many respects the peace-maintainers strain against structures that cannot fit in with a fluid, numerous, better communicating mankind that is increasingly organized, if at all, more outside the reach of government. The improvised modes of organization of peace-maintenance and its humanitarian partners probably point to groping ways needed to reform the basis of governmental cooperation as well as governmental policies. Profound, reverent respect for sovereignty probably does not fit in with humanitarian ideals and human rights standards in large parts of the world.

That congruence was certainly missing in Somalia, Rwanda, Afghanistan and Cambodia.

To expect wholesale reform of the state system in the short term would probably be as utopian as to expect governments, international organizations and NGOs to line up in a tidy rank to meet all complex humanitarian disasters. More muddling through is a more likely prospect. To say so does not in the least detract from efforts to learn from past experience, to build better relationships, to foster organizational congruence and understanding among officials, to seek better methods, to re-examine assumptions and all the rest of the responses detailed in the following chapters.

NOTES

1. For a keen, extended treatment of these issues, see Thomas G. Weiss and Cindy Collins, *Humanitarian Challenges and Intervention: World Politics and Dilemmas of Help*, Boulder, CO: Westview Press, 1996.
2. For a useful attempt at defining peace-maintenance, see Jarat Chopra, 'Introducing Peace Maintenance', *Global Governance*, Vol.4, No.1 (Jan.–Mar. 1998), pp.19–40. This issue of *Global Governance* contains thoughtful articles on various contemporary aspects of maintaining peace.
3. Antonio Donini, 'Asserting Humanitarianism in Peace-Maintenance', *Global Governance*, Vol.4, No.1 (Jan.–Mar. 1998), pp.81–7.
4. See conceptual analysis and case material in Thomas Weiss and Leon Gordenker (eds), *NGOs, the UN & Global Governance*, Boulder, CO: Lynne Rienner, 1996.
5. For examples and analysis, see Thomas G. Weiss (ed.), *Beyond UN Subcontracting: Task-sharing with Regional Security Arrangements and Service-providing NGOs*, Basingstoke: Macmillan Press Ltd., 1998.
6. Leon Gordenker, 'NGOs: The People's Voice in International Governance', University Lecture 15, Tokyo: United Nations University, 1997.
7. That is what scholars of international organization call functionalism. See David Mitrany, *A Working Peace System*, Chicago: Quadrangle Books, 1966 for the argument that most influenced the founders of the UN system.
8. Among the vast literature on human rights, for a treatment of its effect in international relations, see David P. Forsythe, *Human Rights and World Politics,* 2nd Edition, Lincoln: University of Nebraska Press, 1989.
9. Jonathan Moore, *The UN and Complex Emergencies: Rehabilitation in Third World Countries*, Geneva: United Nations Research Institute for Social Development, 1966, pp.4–5; Weiss and Collins, (see n.1), pp.40–68.
10. For a critique of the lack of a critical dimension in these proceedings, see Leon Gordenker, *The UN Tangle: Policy Formation, Reform, and Reorganization*, Cambridge, MA: World Peace Foundation, 1996. A complete list of reform proposals and documents can be found on the Internet in 'United Nations Reform: A Selected Bibliography' maintained by Peter Hajnal at http:///www.library/yale/edu/UN/Unhome/htm.
11. UN Document A/51/1950, 16 July 1997.

Peacekeeping and Refugee Relief

KATHLEEN NEWLAND AND
DEBORAH WALLER MEYERS

The evolution of the role of the UN High Commissioner for Refugees (UNHCR) is traced through its involvement in conflict zones, direct operational relations with military forces and its assumption of responsibility for internally displaced persons and wider humanitarian leadership. The costs and benefits of these changes are examined with particular reference to the war in the former Yugoslavia. Although considerable benefits to the recipients of UNHCR's care are identified, the risks and dilemmas inherent in the perception of a compromised neutrality or impartiality are also highlighted. The dilemmas will almost certainly persist, unless 'militarized humanitarianism' is rendered moot by the increasing reluctance of states to commit to uncertain and risky interventions in conflict-ridden states.

During the course of the 1990s, the Office of the UN High Commissioner for Refugees has increasingly often found itself working in war zones. When not in the midst of an actual combat zone like former Yugoslavia 1992–96, its operations have frequently been on the fringes of armed conflict or dealing with its immediate aftermath. One result is a change in the organization's case load. Today, fewer than half of the roughly 28 million 'persons of concern' to UNHCR are refugees – as defined by the 1951 Convention relating to the Status of Refugees, which specifies that refugees are people who are seeking protection *outside* their own countries. The rest are either internally displaced, recently returned from countries of asylum, or otherwise 'war-affected'. A second result is that UNHCR more often finds itself involved with UN and regional peacekeeping forces who are overseeing the terms of ceasefires or more comprehensive peace agreements (many specifically including the return of refugees). In exceptional cases, most notably that of former Yugoslavia, the UN peacekeeping force is specifically mandated to protect the delivery of humanitarian assistance for which, in Yugoslavia, UNHCR was the lead agency.

Kathleen Newland is a Senior Associate and Deborah Waller Meyers is an Associate in the International Migration Policy Program at the Carnegie Endowment for International Peace.

From Parallel Tracks to Direct Engagement

While UNHCR's involvement with peacekeeping has increased, refugee protection and relief operations have most commonly run parallel to peacekeeping actions rather than working with them directly. In many cases, this is because the peacekeeping force was working within a country and the refugees within UNHCR's mandate were outside the country. This was the case in the early stages of the crisis in Somalia in 1992, for example, when UNHCR's presence was confined to neighbouring countries, chiefly Kenya and Ethiopia, where refugees were concentrated.[1] In Rwanda, similarly, UNHCR was not active inside the country in a major way at the time (early 1994) when the Security Council gave the UN Assistance Mission for Rwanda the responsibility (but not the means) to facilitate and provide security for humanitarian relief operations.[2] By the time the trickle of repatriation to Rwanda turned into a flood, in December 1996, UNAMIR's mandate had expired.

In many other cases, such as Cambodia or Mozambique, when the time came for refugee repatriation, military issues were largely settled. UNHCR's mandate overlapped directly with that of peacekeeping forces only in relatively narrow and specific areas such as demobilization and the reintegration of soldiers. The possibility of repatriation was often conditional on the presence of peacekeepers and the general atmosphere of security they provided, but UNHCR did its tasks while the peacekeepers did theirs, more or less independently. Thus, for example, UNHCR did not have formal relationships with either ONUCA (the UN Observer Group in Central America) after the end of the war in Nicaragua, or with UNTAG (the UN Transition Assistance Group) overseeing the dismantling of South African control over Namibia, even though the agreements these operations were supervising included substantial refugee repatriation. UNHCR field offices communicated with their UN military counterparts, but did not seek military support for repatriation operations. Even the massive UN Transitional Authority in Cambodia, which had repatriation as one of its seven major components, kept UNHCR and the peacekeeping forces at arm's length from each other. The Force Commander was not mandated to give substantial support to UNHCR, and the peacekeepers did not operate on the Thai side of the border where the ambitious repatriation was organized. For UNHCR, the distance was a distinct advantage: even as UN peacekeepers came into conflict with Khmer Rouge forces that refused to carry through the terms of the peace agreement, UNHCR was able to continue its work in Khmer Rouge-controlled territory.

Even with relatively limited direct engagement, the presence of peacekeepers has of course affected the general operating environment for

UNHCR whenever the two are operating in the same country – for better or for worse. It was certainly for the better in El Salvador, where many humanitarians argued against the early withdrawal of ONUSAL because the stabilizing presence of the blue helmets facilitated the conditions for refugee repatriation. In worse cases, on the other hand, the actions of peacekeeping forces may increase refugee flows, even if their military goals are reasonable. The refugee exodus from Sierra Leone in the first half of 1998 (which numbered about 182,000 to Guinea and 55,000 to Liberia) intensified after rebel forces were ousted from the capital in February by the West African peacekeeping force ECOMOG. The rebels' retreat inflicted a murderous campaign of looting, maiming and raping on the civilian population. Many civilians died before reaching the border, succumbing to rebel-inflicted atrocities, diseases contracted in the bush while hiding from rebel forces, or malnutrition. The interior of Sierra Leone was inaccessible to UNHCR for security reasons.[3]

In general, however, the connection between UNHCR and peacekeeping operations has grown more direct during the 1990s. In part, this reflects the changing role of UNHCR as major donor governments have changed their attitudes towards conflict-induced displacements. Determined not to accept heavy caseloads of refugees, they have mandated UNHCR to become involved within refugee-producing countries rather than waiting for refugees to appear at the borders and airports of other countries. Even in the absence of the 'threat' of refugee arrivals, international attention to the plight of internally displaced people has intensified in recent years.

With no other UN organization mandated to deal with the internally displaced, UNHCR's mandate has been expanded in a number of situations to cover them, as well as returnees or war-affected populations. With 'in-country protection' becoming the norm, and with a related drive towards early repatriation, UNHCR now often finds itself working to prevent or contain refugee flows in zones of active conflict or in countries where the ink is scarcely dry on a ceasefire agreement before refugee repatriation begins. In these circumstances, peacekeeping operations are increasingly germane to UNHCR's work, and vice versa.

The remarkable growth of large, complex peacekeeping operations in the early 1990s also explains why UNHCR has been more closely involved with peacekeepers. Most of the large-scale refugee repatriations of the 1990s have taken place in the context of comprehensive peace plans in which peacekeeping forces have played some role. A small number of ventures into peace enforcement – in Somalia, northern Iraq and especially Yugoslavia – involved major humanitarian and military operations running simultaneously. Between 1988 and 1994, military and police personnel deployed by the United Nations rose from under 10,000 to about 75,000.

The cost of UN peacekeeping operations in 1993 surpassed the total of the previous 48 years.[5] More and more of these resources are being devoted to what Rosalyn Higgins characterized as 'ancillary functions' to basic peacekeeping, such as humanitarian relief, human rights monitoring, preparation and supervision of elections and so forth.[6] The expansion of the functions of peacekeeping into tasks that have brought closer working relations with UNHCR and other humanitarian actors has proved controversial, with some voices arguing that the ambitions imposed on peacekeepers by the Security Council have outstripped their capabilities.[7] By 1993, former UN Under-Secretary for Peacekeeping Marrack Goulding described six different kinds of peacekeeping operations, only one of which was of the traditional ceasefire-monitoring, buffer-zone-patrolling type.[8]

UNHCR's decade of engagement with the military began not with a peacekeeping operation but with the establishment of a safe area for the Kurds in northern Iraq. The Security Council authorized the victorious Coalition Forces from the Gulf War to deploy in Northern Iraq for humanitarian purposes, without the consent of the government of Iraq. Later, UNHCR was asked to become the lead agency for humanitarian relief. Although UNHCR entered northern Iraq with the consent of the Iraqi government, the operation represented a major departure. It was a humanitarian mission almost completely detached from UNHCR's traditional protection function. Indeed, the humanitarian operation in northern Iraq was necessary because of Turkey's refusal to admit Kurdish refugees to its territory, where UNHCR might have assumed a more traditional role well away from the contested area within Iraq. Debate within and outside the organization focused on the propriety of UNHCR assuming the lead on humanitarian assistance for internally displaced people, in the wake of a military *fait accompli* that violated the sovereignty of Iraq and denied the Kurds access to international protection. But the agency came to the pragmatic conclusion that it must do all it could to help people in dire need of assistance, even at the cost of compromising on doctrine. This set the stage for an era in which UNHCR would find itself working, often in a leading role, in virtually all the major humanitarian emergencies of the 1990s, often in close cooperation with UN or other military forces.

In the early stages of the operation in northern Iraq, relations between the refugee agency and the Coalition Forces were fraught with tension, with multiple differences on principles, timing of repatriation and operating styles. Both sides came to recognize that the lack of communications between them made their respective tasks more difficult. Northern Iraq marked the beginning of a more conscious attempt by military forces and UNHCR to learn how to work together. But it was the conflict in former

Yugoslavia that truly revolutionized the relationship between UNHCR and military. This time, however, the soldiers wore blue helmets.

Former Yugoslavia: the Turning Point

Fighting broke out in Yugoslavia shortly after Slovenia and Croatia declared their independence in June 1991. In October of that year, UNHCR was asked by the UN Secretary-General to assist displaced persons. Few people could have foreseen what was to come. By the end of 1993, close to 4.3 million people were displaced or seriously affected by war in the former Yugoslavia. Germany had already received nearly 300,000 refugees from the region. UNHCR as the lead humanitarian agency came under considerable criticism for seeming to accommodate the desire of the donor countries to see that these people remained in or close to their homes. In fact, the extremely intransigent attitude of the West Europeans (and other countries further afield who regarded the war as a European problem) considerably narrowed UNHCR's freedom of action in Bosnia.

Unwilling either to intervene militarily in order to end the war or to receive more of its victims, external powers supported an enormous humanitarian effort in the region. Having virtually closed the asylum option, they tried to expand humanitarian relief *in situ*. The Bosnian Serbs and Croats, however, were uncooperative. The logic of the relief effort, to enable people to stay in their homes, was diametrically opposed to the war aim of ethnic homogeneity. By October 1992, Serb forces controlled nearly 70 per cent of the country. Sarajevo and several other towns were under siege.

Relief efforts had been harassed and obstructed from the time of their initiation. In May 1992, for example, a UNHCR convoy had to 'negotiate its way through 90 roadblocks between Zagreb and Sarajevo, many of them manned by undisciplined and drunken soldiers of indeterminate political affiliation'.[9] That same month, a delegate of the International Committee of the Red Cross (ICRC) was killed as his convoy came under mortar fire on the outskirts of Sarajevo, and 11 UNHCR trucks were hijacked.

After the incidents of May 1992, both organizations suspended operations in Bosnia, recognizing that humanitarian space in the conflict had been reduced to the vanishing point. The relief impasse in Bosnia prompted a decision by the Security Council to provide military protection to the humanitarian effort, a decision with profound consequences not only for assistance in Bosnia and the role of UNHCR but also for the course of the war. In June, the Security Council authorized a reinforcement of UNPROFOR, the UN peacekeeping force that was deployed in Croatia in early 1992 following a ceasefire in the Serb–Croat war. It was given the task of ensuring the operation and security of the Sarajevo airport and the delivery of humanitarian assistance to the city. In July, the Sarajevo airlift (which became the longest humanitarian airlift in history) began.

In September 1992, the Council again extended UNPROFOR's mandate to include protection of the delivery of humanitarian assistance throughout Bosnia. UNPROFOR continued to operate under peacekeeping rules of engagement: it could use force only in self-defence, not to accomplish its mission. This seemed paradoxical, to say the least, and created many frustrations. Some within UNHCR expected that a military force would do more to enforce humanitarian norms. The Bosnian Muslims expected UNPROFOR to protect them from violence as well as denial of aid. The Serbs saw the deployment as the UN taking up arms against them.

The deployment of UN troops did not solve the problem of obstruction of relief, and there are those who question whether it intensified the dangers. By the time its mission ended in December 1995 some 210 UNPROFOR soldiers had been killed in Bosnia and Croatia, along with many relief workers. The casualty rates were higher in escorted convoys than non-escorted convoys.

The humanitarian space in Bosnia continued to narrow throughout the next three years. A dramatic turn for the worse came in April 1993 with the breakdown of the Muslim–Croat alliance, which brought ethnic cleansing and siege, previously the province of the Bosnian Serb forces, to areas contested by Muslims and Croats in Central Bosnia and further south around Mostar. In addition, the state of Sarajevo and the besieged enclaves of eastern Bosnia deteriorated as people used up nutritional reserves, and the public infrastructure of the cities – including water, sewage, power services and hospitals – was destroyed by artillery fire. Snipers and mortar fire killed many civilians directly.

From the outset, the violent resistance of the strongest party in the conflict – the Serbs – to humanitarian relief, made the relief operation extraordinarily difficult and dangerous. By early 1993, all three parties were trying to manipulate humanitarian assistance for their own advantage and were obstructing delivery of supplies to 'enemy' populations. This context was uncharted territory for UNHCR. It had no previous experience of operating in the midst of an active war zone; its staff were not trained or knowledgeable in such conditions. ICRC was much more experienced, but it too was blocked and attacked. International norms of humanitarian assistance assumed that all parties to a conflict would recognize humanitarian activities as non-political and consent to them. In former Yugoslavia, the assumptions did not hold.

UNHCR and UNPROFOR responded to the obstruction of humanitarian relief with a combination of persistence, negotiation, threat (rarely carried out), and the non-aggressive use of UNPROFOR military assets. The presence of armed escorts to the humanitarian convoys highlighted the unmistakable fact that the humanitarian mission was no longer operating within the normal ground rule of consent of the parties. The parties, though unwilling to explicitly oppose humanitarian assistance, did in fact oppose it when it helped to sustain the very populations they were trying to eliminate. The tactics of obstruction were endless delays, fruitless negotiations, outright blockades and, sometimes, attacks. Some areas, such as the eastern enclave of Srebrenica, were cut off for many months at a time.

UNHCR and its operating partners made persistent attempts to get through the obstructions peaceably. Some observers have claimed that theft, appropriation and 'tolls' on the assistance meant that no more than about 50 per cent of the relief supplies got through to the intended beneficiaries, but UNHCR insists that the true losses from convoys that crossed front lines were no more than about 10 per cent. When repeated attempts to get through to needy populations by land convoys failed, UNHCR often responded by trying to get around the obstructions physically, often by air. The Sarajevo airlift was the major manifestation of this, but the increasingly desperate condition of the besieged eastern enclaves prompted airdrops of supplies to these areas in the spring and summer of 1993.

As the war went on, the people at greatest risk from both shelling and deprivation of food and medicine were the civilian populations of besieged cities. The difficulty of supplying them brought the UN to perhaps its most crucial operational response to the obstruction of relief. UNHCR reported in March 1993 that 30–40 people were dying every day in the most vulnerable enclave, Srebrenica, and they began an extremely dangerous series of evacuations from the town. In April, the Security Council declared Srebrenica to be a 'safe area', and in May gave five additional towns that designation, including Sarajevo. It asked for additional troops to be assigned for their protection. In June the Council invoked Chapter VII of the UN Charter, and authorized UNPROFOR to take 'necessary measures' to deter attacks and insure protection.

The basis of the 'safe area' in humanitarian law and tradition is that it is not a military resource, yet the Bosnian safe areas were not fully demilitarized. In the eyes of the Serbs, this fact aligned the peacekeepers, and by association the humanitarian agencies, more firmly with the Bosnian Muslim side. From that point on, and especially after February 1994 when NATO air power was invoked for the first time, confrontation between UNPROFOR and the Serbs intensified. This arguably reduced humanitarian options further, as the peacekeeping troops became virtual – and often literal – hostages to the threat of retaliation should stronger measures be taken either to break the blockades against humanitarian deliveries or to protect the safe areas. Their commanders' reluctance to call for NATO close air support, for fear of retaliation against their troops, is often blamed for the success of the Serb assault on Srebrenica in July 1995, which led to the massacre of over 7000 men.

The war in former Yugoslavia raised profound questions about the neutrality of humanitarian efforts. The civilian victims of the war were, especially in the early stages, victims of Serb attack and siege (as was also true in the war in Croatia which had first brought UNHCR into the region). It was therefore difficult not to take sides. Solidarity with the Muslims was encouraged by the US government portrayal of them as the innocent victims of the war; this fed a large appetite in the West for solidarity. This impulse was magnified in the western media, and did not go unnoticed by the Serbs, already disbelieving of the neutrality principle. European governments struggled to condemn the sin but remain neutral towards the sinner. UNHCR also struggled, and continued its work with the displaced throughout the former Yugoslavia, including those in Serbia. Even so, UNHCR was widely perceived by Serbs as an ally of the Muslims.

The neutrality of the humanitarian effort was most severely compromised by the dynamic of the 'safe areas' strategy adopted by the United Nations in May 1993, in an echo of northern Iraq. The plan to protect civilians in the six Muslim towns surrounded by Serb artillery (and, in most cases by Serb-held territory) was to threaten the use of air strikes against the Serb weapons if they were used against the towns. However, the fact that the six enclaves were not demilitarized set up powerful new incentives to abuse the humanitarian purpose of the safe areas. As Susan Woodward described it,

> The Bosnian government turned the safe areas into bases for rest, recuperation and resupply of troops within 'enemy' territory that it hoped to regain and for bases from which to fire out of their enclave into Serbian-claimed territory. The aim of the latter was to provoke Serbian artillery fire to invoke the use of air power against the Serbs and to use the media attention and test of UN and NATO credibility that safe areas would attract to reinforce their propaganda strategy of being the victims of Serb aggression and deserving military assistance. To Bosnian Serbs, the purpose of these enclaves was not humanitarian but strategic... In targeting the safe areas, however, they found an excuse within the humanitarian concept – that if a safe area was not in fact demilitarized but rather an active Bosnian government military installation, they could attack it to provoke international attention. Even if they risked being bombed, they could thereby exert pressure on the UN to create an exclusion zone that would be more likely to demilitarize the area in fact.[10]

Woodward goes on to argue that the Western stance towards the war in Bosnia amounted to a false humanitarianism: that defining the problem strictly in humanitarian rather than political terms aggravated humanitarian problems; and, further, that militarization of the humanitarian effort encouraged Muslims to believe that military intervention on their behalf would eventually come. UNHCR, by being so closely identified with UNPROFOR, was associated in many instances with the effort to protect the Muslims and with the failure to do so. The debate continues, within the agency and beyond it, about the gains in access and the losses in perceived neutrality from its experience with UNPROFOR in former Yugoslavia. Whatever the difficulties, the humanitarian effort did manage to bring sustenance to nearly half the population of Bosnia.

UNHCR and Non-UN Peacekeeping Forces

UNHCR has worked in close proximity to non-UN, regional peacekeeping forces in three settings: Tajikistan, Liberia and Georgia. In the first two, UNHCR has had no formal relationship with the peacekeepers, but its work was affected by the overall security situation in which the regional troops were significant players. The force in Tajikistan was agreed to by the Commonwealth of Independent States but was in effect a Russian force. Its role was closer to peace enforcement than conventional peacekeeping, but its presence made possible the return of refugees and internally displaced people from the Tajik civil war that followed the break-up of the Soviet Union. In Liberia, the Economic Community of West African States fielded a peacekeeping 'monitoring group' which became known as ECOMOG. It was dominated by Nigerian troops and commanders. In both cases, the dominant power in the force entered with its own political agenda. The CIS force had the power to impose its agenda, however, while ECOMOG became in effect another party to the conflict without the means to enforce its will.

Georgia may be the only country in the world to have two independent peacekeeping forces operating simultaneously. One, under the auspices of the Organization for Security and Cooperation in Europe monitors the conflict in South Ossetia. The other, the focus of this discussion, deals with the conflict between Georgia and the breakaway region of in Abkhazia. It is composed of a CIS peacekeeping force, to which Russia is the only troop contributor, and is in turn monitored by the UN Observer Mission in Georgia. UNHCR has a unique relationship with the CISPKF/UNOMIG operation, as it was one of the parties to the agreement that established the mandate for the force. This was contained in the 1994 Quadripartite Agreement on the Voluntary Return of Refugees and Displaced Persons, which was signed by representatives of Georgia, Abkhazia, Russia and UNHCR. It was intended to establish a framework for the return of about 285,000 people displaced from Abkhazia in 1992–93, and made repatriation contingent upon the deployment of an international peacekeeping force. Georgia's call for a UN force beyond the tiny UNOMIG (55 members had been authorized but only 21 were deployed at the time the Agreement was signed) went unanswered. Russian troops filled the vacuum, but their neutrality was always in doubt.

The repatriation effort met with considerable obstruction by the Abkhaz authorities throughout 1994; by the end of the year only 311 displaced persons had returned under the terms of the Agreement. The peacekeeping forces have done little to create conditions conducive to return, although they did stabilize the border region between Abkhazia and the rest of Georgia sufficiently that tens of thousands of people returned spontaneously. UNHCR helped them rebuild their houses but was able to offer little protection. In May 1998, the area of return was attacked by Abkhaz militias. Most of the returnees were forced to flee again. The CISPKF and UNOMIG have not provided police protection to the inhabitants of the region, and have interpreted their humanitarian mandates narrowly. UNHCR conducts joint patrols with the CISPKF in the border region because the area is too dangerous for it to move on its own. Otherwise it receives little direct help from the peacekeeping forces.[11]

The Ups and Downs of Military Support

In former Yugoslavia and other settings, UNHCR has learned that there are both advantages and disadvantages to working closely with peacekeeping forces. The military can provide vital forms of support to UNHCR. They include the creation of a more secure environment, direct defence of humanitarian assets and personnel, and humanitarian support activities (specific tasks undertaken in support of a humanitarian operation, such as escorting convoys, transporting humanitarian supplies and equipment, providing security for humanitarian personnel, repairing and maintaining infrastructure and the like). Even under the most restrictive rules of engagement, peacekeeping forces have a mandate to use force to defend themselves and UN personnel. Against these assets must be weighed the costs of being closely associated with peacekeeping, which may include a perceived loss of neutrality, high expenses and loss of control over operations.

Humanitarian personnel, accustomed to working under principles of consent, continue to feel ambivalent about working under military escort. The ICRC has almost always refused to do so. UNHCR, however, concluded in former Yugoslavia and other settings that the ability to access areas that would otherwise be off-limits was worth the risk of being perceived as less than neutral. In other words, the most important consideration was that desperately needed assistance should get through to people who might otherwise have perished.

The decision to work with the military does not make the fact of collaboration easy. Differences in style, costs, control, timing and notions of acceptable risk between UNHCR and the national military establishments that contributed peacekeeping forces have surfaced in headquarters and the field. Distinct organizational cultures account for some of the friction than has occurred in relations between UNHCR and peacekeeping forces. Differences in command structure can be particularly frustrating to the military, which is used to operating in a field structure where all functions report to and take orders from a commander in the field. As a UNHCR training manual explains, UNHCR functions in the field (such as administration, public information, programming, supply and transport, and protection) are more autonomous; the head of a UNHCR field operation does not necessarily give them their orders. Peacekeeping forces may not find a single, unitary point of contact for UNHCR who can speak with authority about all aspects of the operation. At the same time, UNHCR field staff may have greater decision-making authority than their military counterparts, who look up the chain of command for policy guidance. UNHCR decision-makers tend to be younger and correspondingly less experienced than their military counterparts.[12]

Perhaps the most glaring difference in the cultures of the military and UNHCR is the value placed on improvisation, which in the military is low. Military organizations work hard to eliminate surprises and standardize responses with a pre-defined goal or 'end-state' in view. UNHCR values improvisation in the field, where resources are almost by definition inadequate to the possible tasks and the challenge is always to stretch them as far as possible. Different notions of accountability therefore prevail.

Issues of control also arise with respect to national military units deployed for humanitarian support. Humanitarian personnel and peacekeepers mandated to protect humanitarian operations may have different views of the degree and nature of threats, and of the best ways to deal with them. Whose professional judgement should prevail in such a case? In Bosnia, the peacekeeping forces supplied briefings to humanitarian personnel on the security situation in a given area on a given day; the decision about whether to proceed was left to the UNHCR field officer. UNHCR employees often found the military to be more cautious than they themselves. There were reportedly many times that the peacekeepers judged it to be too dangerous to move but the humanitarian operations went ahead without them, in a strange inversion of the usual perception of risk-taking preparedness between soldier and civilian. The great reluctance of military and civilian authorities in the West to risk the lives of soldiers has led some to question the value of peacekeeping contingents that devote an overwhelming proportion of their energy and resources to self-defence.

The high cost of military involvement in humanitarian operations is also a constraint on cooperation. The logistical miracles that a well-equipped military force can accomplish do not come cheap, nor do the well-trained soldiers and sophisticated equipment. In 1993, the UN Under-Secretary-General for Humanitarian Affairs complained that 'only US$1 was being spent on humanitarian assistance for every US$10 spent on the military peace-enforcement operation' in Somalia.[13] Military support for humanitarian operations is almost always the most expensive option – but in some cases it may be the only realistic option to accomplish a particular task like breaking the siege of a civilian population.

Under current arrangements, peacekeeping troops are not only expensive but also extremely slow to deploy. The pace of humanitarian emergencies has frequently outrun them – most notably in the case of the Rwandan genocide. By the time the Security Council authorized UNAMIR to expand its troop strength, in mid-May 1994, more than 200,000 people had already been killed. Reinforcements did not arrive until the genocide had taken more than half a million lives and had been halted only by the military victory of the Rwanda Patriotic Front. The speed necessary to keep up with the pace of a massive humanitarian emergency has not been available from multilateral peacekeeping operations, but in fact has to date been supplied only by national forces deployed by individual member states or small coalitions. This was the case when Coalition Forces went in to northern Iraq, when French forces established a 'safe zone' in southwest Rwanda, and when US troops were deployed in Operation *Support Hope* to assist UNHCR in coping with record-breaking arrivals of Rwandan refugees in Zaire in July 1994.

By contrast, a new peacekeeping operation would take three to four months at best from Security Council request to initial deployment. First a budget must be drawn up, approved by the UN Advisory Committee on Administrative and Budgetary Questions, and sent to the Fifth Committee of the General Assembly. It normally takes six to eight weeks for assessments to be sent to member governments; they have 30 days to pay but usually take longer. Procurement and transport can drag on for months.[14] UNHCR, by contrast, has developed its emergency response capacity and can be in the field within days of a crisis erupting. It has been able to accomplish objectives such as pre-positioning of supplies, stand-by arrangements for personnel and equipment from certain governments, and rapid response units that so far have been denied to the UN Department of Peacekeeping Operations. The early days of a refugee emergency are often the most dangerous, and yet the early days are when UNHCR is least likely to have the protection of a multilateral peacekeeping force.

Despite problems associated with culture, cost, speed and so forth, UNHCR has welcomed the collaboration with peacekeeping forces. Working to implement the repatriation and reintegration components of comprehensive peace plans as in Cambodia, El Salvador and Mozambique, UNHCR has benefited from the improved security environment that peacekeepers help to establish. Specific activities such as quartering of demobilized troops, demining, repair of essential infrastructure and collection of weapons have made refugee return safer. In some instances, peacekeeping troops have participated directly in repatriation operations, accompanying convoys of returnees, guarding reception centres and monitoring the welfare of returning refugees.[15]

Operating in the midst of armed conflict places UNHCR in a different relationship with peacekeeping forces, one in which it may be much more dependent on the logistical resources and defensive capacity of the military units. UNHCR officials have often said that their partnership with UNPROFOR allowed them to reach hundreds of thousands of people at risk in Bosnia, through operations such as the Sarajevo airlift, air drops to the eastern enclaves and convoys with military escorts. The High Commissioner now employs a military advisor, and there have been several periods when national military officers were seconded to UNHCR during airlift or other military operations.

From the early days of Operation *Provide Comfort*, when a reluctant UNHCR took over from Coalition Forces it resented for supporting Turkey's refusal to give asylum to the Kurds, UNHCR has learned much about working with the military, and vice versa. Both have taken the relationship seriously and devoted considerable resources to learning each other's strengths, weaknesses and values. Joint training, lessons learned exercises, personnel exchanges and field manuals have proliferated in the 1990s. Soldiers and humanitarian workers have learned to respect each other's particular brand of professionalism. Consultation, coordination and communication have become standard operating procedures, despite the substantial differences that will and should remain.

The Problem of Maintaining Neutrality

The authorization of military force to deliver humanitarian assistance in the context of a Chapter VII, UN peace-enforcement operation is a contradiction in terms if one accepts the time-honoured rhetoric of neutrality and impartiality of humanitarian assistance. The statute of UNHCR insists that the High Commissioner's work is of a strictly non-political character. But a Chapter VII action is inherently and unmistakably political. This does not mean that military forces should never be deployed to provide humanitarian assistance. Rather, if the consent of parties to the conflict cannot be obtained, such assistance should not be provided by the same forces that are carrying out political tasks on behalf of the Security Council – if the sponsoring governments are serious about the neutral character of the humanitarian effort. If not, they should put the humanitarian effort explicitly on the political agenda and be prepared to back it up with the necessary force.

The late Fred Cuny wrote with considerable prescience in 1991 (before the start of the Yugoslav conflict) that 'One of the most important determinants of the success of a military deployment in a humanitarian operation is whether or not the force is able to assume and maintain a "mantle of neutrality". The importance of this cannot be overstated. If at any time one or more parties to a conflict perceive that a foreign force has other than humanitarian objectives, either for itself or for the other party, the operation in which it is involved will be regarded as a military intervention and the force will become engaged in the conflict. Once the mantle of neutrality is lost, it cannot be regained.'[16]

The experience of former Yugoslavia demonstrates that when the United Nations sanctions the use of force against one party to a conflict, it destroys the perceived impartiality and neutrality of the UN mission as a whole, including the humanitarian organizations associated with the operation. The same is largely true when force is threatened. Parties to a conflict sometimes differentiate between the 'good UN', which brings humanitarian assistance to vulnerable people, and the 'bad UN' which imposes sanctions or sends troops to interfere with the war fighting tactics of one or more of the belligerents. UNHCR has, in maintaining a distance from UN-approved or sponsored military forces, in some cases managed to maintain good relations with parties, such as the Khmer Rouge (during the UNTAC period) and the government of Iraq (during Operation *Provide Comfort*) that were sharply at odds with the political bodies of the United Nations. The more closely UNHCR works with forces that are involved in enforcement actions (Chapter VII), the more likely it is to be categorized as 'bad UN'. UNPROFOR may have exhibited the worst of both worlds, drawing the ire of the Bosnian Serbs (and intermittently, the Bosnian Croats) as it compromised the neutrality of the humanitarian effort in their eyes, but failing to enforce access to populations in need of assistance because of its unwillingness to use force to fulfil its mandate.

Conclusion

In both former Yugoslavia and Rwanda, UN member states have been willing to empower peacekeeping forces to protect humanitarian assistance to threatened civilians but not to protect the civilians from violence. Even with respect to assistance, they have not been willing to recognize that delivering humanitarian assistance to civilians in the teeth of opposition from a party to conflict is much more like war than like traditional peacekeeping. They therefore have not altered the rules of engagement sufficiently to make humanitarian support operations effective. As former British army officer John Mackinlay observes, 'Militarily, a humanitarian support force is a much more sophisticated operation to mount and command than a traditional peace force. Peacekeeping forces are normally static garrisons; by comparison, a relief escort column is an operation of war.'[17]

It may indeed be a misnomer to incorporate humanitarian support operations in armed conflict under the rubric of peacekeeping. As Special Assistant to the UN Secretary-General, Shashi Tharoor (a veteran of the UN Department of Peace-Keeping Operations, as is his boss) noted, after the Cold War ended, '"Peacekeeping" became a catch-all term covering not merely the monitoring and implementation of ceasefire agreements, but an entire range of tasks including supervising and running elections, upholding human rights, overseeing land reform, delivering humanitarian aid under fire, rebuilding failed states as well as trying to impose peace on adversaries not yet willing to lay down their arms.'[18] Altered tasks for peacekeepers should logically have led to altered rules of engagement – but in most cases did not. It was clear, for example, that humanitarian support of the kind needed, for example, in Zaire in 1996–97, could not be accomplished with only a light self-defence mandate. UNHCR, along with a number of governments, called at that time for a humanitarian intervention force rather than a peacekeeping force. It is notable, however, that the international community was not able to agree on the deployment of such a force.

A traditional peacekeeping mandate, with all its limitations, may be the maximum that states will permit by way of military support for humanitarian efforts. The United States, with the largest assessment to the UN peacekeeping budget, has demonstrated increasing reluctance to authorize even that much. UNHCR may have learned the lessons of working with peacekeepers in former Yugoslavia only to find that it has nowhere in future to apply them.

NOTES

1. In September, 1992, UNHCR was asked to explore cross-border relief operations that would permit refuges to return home, or permit those who had not yet fled to stay home, in circumstances where lack of food was their only reason for fleeing. UNHCR's presence within Somalia was concentrated near the Kenyan border, mostly in southern Somalia, and still did not bring it into close operational contact with the urban-based peacekeeping forces. The repatriation effort did, of course, benefit to the extent that the peacekeeping forces helped to establish a more secure environment in the countryside.
2. Between late 1994 and late 1996, UNHCR did have staff working in Rwanda to assist and monitor the security and welfare of returning refugees and internally displaced people. They worked with UNAMIR and UN human rights monitors deployed by the UN High Commissioner for Human Rights.
3. UNHCR News Release of 2 June 1998. ECOMOG operates less as a traditional peace-keeping force than as a party to the conflicts both in Liberia and Sierra Leone.
4. See Roberta Cohen and Francis M. Deng, *Masses in Flight: The Global Crisis of Internal Displacement*, Washington, DC: The Brookings Institution, 1998 for a review of the issue of internal displacement and the work of the Secretary-General's Special Representative on internally displaced persons.
5. UNHCR, *The State of the World's Refugees: In Search of Solutions*, New York: Oxford University Press, 1995, p.98.
6. Rosalyn Higgins, 'The New United Nations and former Yugoslavia', in *International Affairs*, Vol.69, No.3 (July 1993), p.469.
7. See Shashi Tharoor, 'Should UN Peacekeeping Go "Back to Basics"?', *Survival*, Vol.37, No.4 (Winter 1995–96), pp.52–64.
8. Marrack Goulding, 'The Evolution of United Nations Peacekeeping', in *International Affairs*, Vol.69, No.3 (Winter 1993), pp.451–64.
9. UN Document. S/23900, quoted in Oliver Ramsbotham and Tom Woodhouse, *Humanitarian Intervention in Contemporary Conflict*, Cambridge: Polity Press, 1996.
10. Susan L. Woodward, *Balkan Tragedy: Chaos and Dissolution after the Cold War*, Washington DC: Brookings Institution, 1995, p.320–21.
11. UNHCR, 'A UNHCR Handbook for the Military on Humanitarian Operations', Geneva, January, 1995, Appendix 1; S. Neil MacFarland, Larry Minear and Stephen D. Shenfield, *Armed conflict in Georgia: A Case Study in Humanitarian Action and Peacekeeping*, Providence: Watson Institute Occasional Paper #21, 1996; UNHCR Briefing Notes, Geneva, 10 July 1998.
12. UNHCR, 'A UNHCR Handbook for the Military on Humanitarian Operations', ibid.
13. Quoted in Hugo Slim and Emma Visman, 'Evacuation, Intervention and Retaliation: United Nations Humanitarian Operations in Somalia, 1991–1993', in John Harriss, (ed.), *The Politics of Humanitarian Intervention*, London: Pinter, 1995, p.160.
14. 'United Nations Peacekeeping: Trotting to the Rescue', *The Economist*, June 25 1994.
15. UNHCR, *The State of the World's Refugees: In Search of* Solution (see n.5).
16. Frederick C. Cuny, 'Dilemmas of Military Involvement in Humanitarian Relief', in Leon Gordenker and Thomas G. Weiss (eds), *Soldiers, Peacekeepers and Disasters*, London: Macmillan for the International Peace Academy, 1991, p.76.
17. John Mackinlay, 'The Role of Military Forces in a Humanitarian Crisis', in Leon Gordenker and Thomas G. Weiss (eds), ibid, p.29.
18. Shashi Tharoor (see n.7).

The World Health Organization and Peacekeeping

YVES BEIGBEDER

Although the World Health Organization has no peacekeeping mandate, it has adopted resolutions condemning instruments of war and introduced a request to the International Court of Justice on the use of nuclear weapons, which was rejected as not within the scope of the organization's activities. Some of WHO's emergency missions are related to peacekeeping. WHO and UNICEF have brokered ceasefires to allow poliomyelitis immunization campaigns to be conducted in countries affected by conflicts. WHO and the Pan American Health Organization launched the 'Health as a Bridge for Peace' initiative in 1984 in Central America and Panama. The concept is now being pursued by the WHO Division of Emergency and Humanitarian Action. However, health is only one of possible causes of conflict and health officials cannot replace political leaders. Support for peace cannot become WHO's primary objective, but WHO activities may support peacekeeping in the organization's own health domain.

The World Health Organization has no mandate to maintain peace and security: that is one of the explicit purposes of the United Nations. However, one part of the preamble of the WHO constitution establishes a link between health and peace: 'The health of all peoples is fundamental to the attainment of peace and security and is dependent upon the fullest cooperation of individuals and states.'

The link between the mandates of most UN specialized agencies and peace was explicitly established in their constitutions in the first attempt to apply the functionalist theory that the creation of autonomous, functional international organizations, specialized in particular fields of activity, would create transnational professional communities which would break, or progressively erode, the principal sources of contention between national sovereignties and thus preserve peace. WHO was to resolve the basic health problems of the world which would, it was hoped, help to extirpate the roots of war. A 1962 resolution of the World Health Assembly (Res. WHA15.51) reaffirmed that the improvement of world health would contribute importantly to peace, while adding in turn that peace was a basic condition

Yves Beigbeder, a former WHO official, is an Adjunct Professor at Webster University in Geneva.

for the preservation and improvement of the health of people in the whole world. The resolution also declared that physicians and all other medical workers have, in the exercise of their profession and through the relief and help they give to their patients, an important role to play in the preservation and promotion of peace, by contributing to the elimination or at least the attenuation of the causes of distress and dissatisfaction.

In spite of these general affirmations, WHO's mandate does not include any direct reference to war and peace or to peacekeeping. Its constitution only refers among many other substantial functions, 'to furnish...in emergencies, necessary aid upon the request or acceptance of governments' (Art.2(d)). Its explicit mandate in this area is therefore limited to emergency relief which may respond to natural or man-made emergencies, including internal and external conflicts.

However, WHO cannot ignore the impact of war on health. Warfare entails killing, the physical and mental maiming of combatants and non-combatants, the destruction of health institutions, the dislocation of health services, the destruction of housing, clean water and food supplies. It may cause famine, malnutrition, environmental contamination, the surge or resurgence of epidemic diseases, the increase of poverty and flows of refugees. In addition to its relief activities, WHO has issued a number of declarations condemning instruments of war, and particularly nuclear weapons. In 1993, WHO submitted a request to the International Court of Justice for an advisory opinion on the use of nuclear weapons.

WHO against Instruments of War

WHO has supported the accession of states to international conventions or protocols prohibiting the use of 'illegal' weapons. Between 1967 and 1970, WHO supported the accession of all states to the Protocol for the Prohibition of the Use in War of Asphyxiating, Poisonous or Other Gases, and of Bacteriological Methods of Warfare, signed in Geneva on 17 June 1925 and emphasized the need for the rapid prohibition of the development, production and stockpiling of chemical and bacteriological (biological) weapons and the destruction of stocks of such weapons as a necessary measure in the fight for human health (Res. WHA20.54 and WHA23.53). In 1979, WHO called for the consolidation of international détente and the attainment of disarmament, so that the released resources could be used for the development of public health in the world. In 1981, WHO referred to the then present aggravation of the international situation and the growing danger of thermonuclear conflict, which would inevitably lead to the irreversible destruction of the environment and the deaths of hundreds of millions of people, as well as grave consequences for the life and health of the populations of all countries and of future generations. However, WHO's only concrete contribution to this mounting threat was the creation of a 'broad and authoritative' international committee composed of eminent experts in medical science and public health to carry out a comprehensive study and elucidation of the threat of thermonuclear war. In 1983, the World Health Assembly noted 'with grave concern' the conclusions of the committee on the effects of nuclear war on health and health services (Res. WHA34.38 and 36.28). Also in 1981, states were requested to clear material war remnants, especially mines (Res. WHA34.39). In 1986, member states were urged by the Assembly to strive for the cessation of the arms race with particular regard to nuclear weapons, and in 1988, the Assembly rejected any embargo on medical supplies for political reasons.

On 14 May 1993, the Assembly requested the International Court of Justice to give an advisory opinion on the following question: 'In view of the health and environmental effects, would the use of nuclear weapons by a state in war or other armed conflict be a breach of its obligations under international law including the WHO Constitution?' This politically-inspired resolution had been adopted by a vote of 73–40, with ten abstentions; 41 states were absent from the voting.

The Court ruled, by 11 to 3, that although the World Health Organization is duly authorized under the UN Charter to request advisory opinions from the ICJ, and the opinion requested concerned a legal question, WHO's request did not relate to a question arising within the scope of the activities of that organization as required under Article 96, paragraph 2 of the UN Charter. WHO's responsibilities are necessarily restricted to the sphere of public health, and cannot encroach on the responsibilities of other parts of the UN system. More specifically, questions concerning the use of force, the regulation of armaments and disarmament are within the competence of the UN and outside that of the specialized agencies. In short, 'keep to your mandate' – advice which may also apply to WHO's activities related to peacekeeping.

In 1994, over the dissent of the nuclear powers, the UN General Assembly asked the Court for an advisory opinion on the question: 'Is the threat or use of nuclear weapons in any circumstance permitted under international law?' The judges found, unanimously, that 'a threat or use of nuclear weapons should be compatible with the requirements of the international law applicable in armed conflict'; however, they split 7–7 on whether the nature of these weapons makes for a general presumption of incompatibility, and they also split on whether it is legal to threaten or use nuclear weapons in an extreme circumstance of self-defence. All agreed on the 'obligation to pursue in good faith' negotiations leading to nuclear disarmament – a political, non-legal, recommendation.

WHO's Emergency Operations

Operational emergency assistance in the health field has long been carried out by such NGOs as the International Committee of the Red Cross, Red Cross and Red Crescent Societies and their Federation, medical associations – Médecins sans Frontières, Médecins du Monde, Quaker Physicians – and, in part, by other humanitarian NGOs such as Save the Children, Oxfam and Caritas. Within the UN system, the main emergency operational assistance (not limited to health) is assured by UNDP (represented in 134 countries), UNICEF (children and mothers), UNHCR (refugees) and WFP (food assistance). Coordination of emergency relief is, in principle, the responsibility of the UN Emergency Relief Coordinator (renamed UN Humanitarian Assistance Coordinator under the Secretary-General's reform proposals of July 1997). The Coordinator chairs the Inter-Agency Standing Committee, the main consultative committee for humanitarian agencies, of which WHO is a member.

The budget of the WHO emergency programme has grown to almost five times its original size between 1988 ($6.3 million) and 1996 ($27.5 million). Consisting of mainly extra-budgetary contributions, it represents almost five per cent of the total WHO budget for 1996.

In the first decades, the programme was limited to providing medical supplies to combat epidemics or other emergencies in response to countries' requests. In 1975, the Assembly encouraged the Director-General to further develop the organization's capacity for providing health assistance to disaster-stricken peoples and to play an active role in the joint relief and rehabilitation efforts undertaken by the UN system and the League of Red Cross Societies with respect to disasters and natural catastrophes (Res. WHA28.45). In the 1970s and early 1980s, WHO's main emergency activity was relief. Gradually, the emphasis was changed to disaster preparedness and response, to include involvement in training, assessment of health situations and needs, and coordination of large-scale disaster operations, mainly through WHO regional offices. A network of collaborating centres was created and the services of consultants were used extensively. An Emergency Relief Unit was set up at WHO headquarters in 1974. It became the Division of Emergency Relief Operations in 1989, then the Division of Emergency and Humanitarian Action in 1993.

In May 1992, the French representative to the Assembly, Dr Bernard Kouchner, the founder of MSF and MDM, felt that WHO should go beyond its traditional mission. It was anomalous that WHO should not be in the front line when faced with emergencies involving major risks to public health. 'Had everybody [UNRWA, UNICEF, UNHCR, FAO] except WHO taken over health problems?' he asked. Kouchner encouraged WHO to play a more dynamic role in the field, particularly in response to humanitarian emergencies. He proposed the creation of a humanitarian 'strike-force', under the immediate authority of the Director-General, backed by an emergency unit in Geneva, with the support of medical volunteers.[1] In January 1994, Dr Hiroshi Nakajima, then Director-General, declared that providing emergency assistance had become a vital function of WHO.

WHO's Current Role in Emergency Humanitarian Assistance

Based on the provision of normative and technical guidance, WHO's cooperation involves:

- fielding specialized teams, either on its own or in cooperation with other agencies, for the assessment of the health aspects of an emergency at its onset or during the course of its evolution;
- provision of emergency health coordinators to improve collaboration, avoid overlap in the provision of assistance and monitor the evolution of the situation;
- provision of specialized supplies and expertise, when necessary;
- preparation, updating and dissemination of appropriate guidelines and protocols relating to the handling of health problems recurrent in emergency situations;
- timely provision of technical and operational leadership in the case of epidemic emergencies or emergencies of a primary public health nature, including early warning systems; and
- setting up of an information system for the early detection of health emergencies.

Emergency preparedness programmes, including training, are carried out at national and regional levels, through WHO regional offices and country representatives' offices – and at the inter-regional level, with other UN organizations. WHO supports the strengthening of the technical capacity of regional and inter-regional emergency preparedness centres. When assessing health needs in an emergency, WHO makes provisions for both emergency action and the rehabilitation of national health structures. Finally, WHO undertakes some responsibility for humanitarian advocacy in the health sector. In this area, WHO intercedes with the responsible authorities for:

- the protection of health personnel and health infrastructure in situations of conflict;
- the protection of non-combatants and effective care of mental and

physical injuries arising from antipersonnel mines and situations of collective violence;
• ease of access and the provision of health assistance to internally displaced persons.

The experience gained from emergencies or from consultation with partners has corroborated the view that the organization's role in such situations is primarily normative in the technical sense of the term, as opposed to the 'hands-on' operational emergency response of other UN agencies which requires massive logistics support and a large number of staff in the field. However, the credibility of its technical guidance and its authority in coordinating health programmes depends for a large part on the effective presence of qualified emergency staff on the spot. The organization must therefore be able to mobilize, at short notice, experts and managers who are both technically qualified and capable of working effectively under emergency conditions.[2]

WHO Emergency Missions and their Relation to Peacekeeping

Some emergency missions have included mainly traditional WHO activities – the dispatch of medical supplies, technical guidance to ministries of health and other organizations, epidemiological assessment and surveillance, disease control or eradication, the rehabilitation of health structures; other missions added to these technical activities 'bridge for peace' efforts – that is, bringing former enemies to work together in health programmes, aiming ultimately at their reconciliation in order to consolidate peace.

Traditional Emergency Missions

Democratic People's Republic of Korea: In 1996, WHO assessed the impact of floods on the health care delivery system and mobilized extra-budgetary funds for flood relief. In addition, $1 million of WHO's regular budget was used to supply urgently needed essential drugs, vitamins and medical supplies.[3]

Liberia: Also in 1996, WHO airlifted by helicopter a consignment of emergency medicines, including surgical supplies for treating the wounded. The WHO representative, who remained in Monrovia throughout the fighting, worked closely with the Ministry of Health, other UN agencies and NGOs to distribute the new supplies to hospitals and health centres in Monrovia and to reorganize emergency services.[4]

Rwanda: Following the 1994 genocide, WHO's initial response was to bring assistance to refugees and displaced populations. WHO's emergency assistance was along traditional technical lines: deploying teams of epidemiologists, primarily along the Zairian border, to identify the precise strain of cholera and other pathogens that had decimated the refugee population and, in the refugee camps at Goma, helping to bring rapidly under control epidemics of cholera, dysentery and meningitis. WHO provided drugs and supplies for the control of these diseases and supported laboratory services. In 1995, WHO pre-positioned stocks of emergency medical supplies in Kigali and dispatched a consignment of cholera kits to Bujumbura on a contingency basis. WHO also worked on the rehabilitation of health services and on the re-establishment of the national epidemiology system. At the request of the Ministry of Health, it made an assessment of the health situation following the massive influx of refugees in 1996. It provided essential drugs and other medical supplies for the control of cholera and malaria and recruited UN volunteer medical officers to provide care in the district health facilities in the communes where there was the greatest influx of refugees.[5]

Sri Lanka: WHO raised extra-budgetary funds for humanitarian action in favour of the population affected by civil conflict and took action in collaboration with the UN Emergency Task Force in improving the flow of medical supplies to the population by standardizing medical supplies and setting up an emergency supplies management system. WHO also trained staff of NGOs providing assistance.

Emergency-cum-Peacekeeping Missions

Afghanistan: In the protracted conflict situation in Afghanistan, WHO's main activities were concerned with emergency relief, disease control and training of health personnel. The provision of essential drugs and the upgrading of hospitals and health services were directed and financed in coordination with a range of partners, including UNHCR and WFP. WHO undertook the physical and functional rehabilitation of a number of health institutions, hospitals and health centres in different regions. This involved the reconstruction or renovation of premises, and the provision of medical and laboratory equipment and supplies and health care documentation. The water supply system in three cities was rehabilitated in collaboration with other UN agencies and NGOs. Public health staff were trained on the interrelationship between water, sanitation and health, and water surveillance and cholera prevention.

In 'bridge to peace' activities, WHO was instrumental with UNICEF in helping obtain a humanitarian ceasefire between warring factions in order to organize an intensive one-week immunization campaign in November 1994, during which almost one million children were vaccinated against poliomyelitis. In addition, almost 350,000 children were vaccinated against measles, and 320,000 women of childbearing age received anti-tetanus vaccination. A second similar immunization campaign was organized from 29 April to 4 May 1995. More than 3.5 million children under the age of five were vaccinated against polio in April and May 1997. WHO has advocated the right of all Afghans – and particularly the right of all Afghan children – to health, and promoted extensive nation-wide social mobilization. WHO also succeeded in negotiating the passage of relief convoys through the military front to besieged Kabul in winter 1996.[6]

Angola: WHO has worked with both the government and UNITA bringing both sides together to deal with health matters and thereby to promote mutual confidence. WHO's work in Angola centred on assistance in the disarmament, quartering, and demobilization of soldiers from government and UNITA forces. After the signing of the Lusaka Protocol in October 1994, WHO played an important role in the development and implementation of the health programme during quartering and demobilization phases. Key activities included: designing common protocols between groups, brokering arrangements for joint data collection activities, working with communities to develop public health programmes, training military health personnel, setting up health units in the quartering areas, development of an agreement for a joint medical team to classify disabilities, and supporting a legal basis for institutionalizing benefits to disabled war victims and demobilized soldiers.

WHO has provided support to both parties through a health transition project funded by the UK Overseas Development Administration and the government of the Netherlands. This project aims at strengthening national capacity in health policy development – the planning, coordination and management of health activities, in particular at the provincial level. In 1996, one emergency health coordinator was seconded to the UN Humanitarian Assistance Coordination Unit to oversee health activities for demobilized soldiers. In collaboration with NGOs, WHO conducted epidemic assessment and training, and provided vaccines to control outbreaks of meningitis. Technical workshops and training classes were provided to health workers of the government and UNITA administrations. The role of WHO was not limited to its health domain. WHO representatives were involved in negotiations with both parties, and in forging legal instruments for the inclusion of the disabled and demobilized ex-combatants. The Ministry of Health, WHO, UNICEF, Rotary International and other NGOs carried out a national polio vaccination campaign in August and September 1996, during which over two million children were vaccinated.

Former Yugoslavia: Besides the wilful attacks on health personnel and health care institutions and the destruction of public utilities vital to health care by parties to the conflict, health personnel were forced (or willing?) to commit unethical acts and/or were prevented from caring for sick and wounded members of enemy parties.

As a response to this problem WHO, jointly with the Norwegian Medical Association with financing from the Norwegian Ministry of Foreign Affairs, convened two meetings of the medical associations of the republics of former Yugoslavia. The first meeting, in September 1993, approved a declaration whereby the participants agreed to use the moral authority of the medical professions to press publicly for action to protect health and prevent disease in the affected countries, to monitor and exchange information on adherence to international law, and to draw the attention of the competent international and national authorities to all violations of human rights. They also agreed:

* to reaffirm the Hippocratic oath that treatment should be given without any discrimination as to race, ethnic group, religion or nationality to all injured civilians and combatants;
* that there should be no hindrance to the supply of essential drugs, vaccines and other medical supplies or interruption of water, energy and other essential services to communities;
* to condemn the violation of health in war and reaffirm the ethical duty of the health professionals and health authorities in Croatia (UN protected areas).

WHO also convened meetings of health authorities in Bosnia-Herzegovina (both Serb- and Croat-controlled) in April 1994 and in September 1996 which agreed upon the same points.

Because of the high prevalence of mental health problems and injuries as a result of armed conflicts, WHO implemented integrated mental and physical rehabilitation programmes, notably in Bosnia-Herzegovina. WHO has assisted health professionals in training, categorising mental health problems and data collection. Emphasis was placed on community-based care rather than costly hospital services. Victims of physical injuries received prostheses, physical therapy and counselling. Other more general activities included assessing health needs, carrying out epidemiological studies, advising health authorities and other organizations on public health matters and the nutritional content of food supplies, supporting health care institutions with medical and other supplies.

Beginning in January 1996, WHO played the role of the principal mediator in health by chairing the Joint Implementation Committee in health in the Eastern Slavonia region of Croatia. Activities undertaken included bringing together Croat and Serb health workers for confidence building, joint technical analysis of the health situation, joint planning and implementation of health activities, and the administrative reintegration of the health sector. Specific activities included developing commissions on administrative reintegration, technical activities in mental health, physical rehabilitation and epidemiology, health research, organizing a sub-national immunization day against polio, and provision of essential drugs.

The strategy behind the initiative was to provide a safe space for dialogue on technical issues, creating the basis for mutual understanding and cooperation within the health sector. This included emphasizing respect for both sides' roles as health professionals, and their traditional neutrality and impartiality in situations of conflict.

However, problems arose in WHO's support for integrating Eastern Slavonian and Croatian health staff into the Croatian health care system and incorporating the population of Eastern Slavonia into the Croatian health insurance system. Distrust on the part of patients and obstruction or intimidation by officials and individuals led to unwillingness to accept services from other ethnic groups. In spite of WHO's efforts, only a few Serb health professionals had been recruited to work under the Croatian administration, and only about 50 per cent of the Serb population was covered by the Croatian National Insurance System. A participant to an international conference on Trauma Recovery Training: Lessons Learned (Zagreb, 13–15 July 1997) wrote that it verges on 'absurdity' to attempt community health or individual mental health recovery so long as prejudice and ethnic hatred are 'institutionalized, even within medical facilities'.

In Kosovo, opposing parties worked together on polio immunization campaigns.

Health and Development for Displaced Populations (Hedip)

Within WHO, Hedip has fostered local peacebuilding action through participative community action in health and health-related sectors. Between 1992 and 1995, Hedip has conducted pilot projects in three conflict-affected countries – Mozambique, Sri Lanka and Croatia – to develop and refine methods for:

• using action in health and health-related sectors to strengthen and encourage reconciliation at the community level;
• providing assistance so that humanitarian and development aid benefits the entire community, not just one specific group;
• facilitating effective local coordination and intersectoral actions;

- bridging the gap between emergency assistance and long-term sustainable development.

Hedip offers experience in participative engagement for conflict reduction.[7]

Health as a Bridge for Peace (HBP)

This evolving concept is based on the premise that shared health concerns can transcend political, economic, social and ethnic divisions, promote dialogue, foster solidarity, and contribute to peace among people. The term 'HBP' was first used by the Pan American Health/WHO Regional Office for the Americas. It was based on PAHO's programme to bring together nations and factions in conflict to plan and implement joint health activities in Central America from 1984 until the early 1990s. The main actors of the programme, besides PAHO, were the governments of El Salvador, Nicaragua, Guatemala, Honduras, Belize and Panama, the OAS, UNICEF, UNFPA, UNDP, the World Bank, bilateral donors and NGOs. The main activities were ministerial-level meetings to assess and plan health activities, joint border monitoring of health threats, vector control, collaborative training exchanges, drug and vaccine exchanges and joint purchases, immunization ceasefires, and government-to-government agreements. In 1984, PAHO and the Ministers of Health of Central America founded the Plan for Priority Health Needs in Central America and Panama. It was hoped that the consensus concerning health problems and the progress in the health sector would serve as a catalyst for other cooperative efforts and thereby strengthen attempts to obtain peace in the war-torn area. Another objective was to mobilize financial support from outside the region to implement critical projects for which national funds were lacking. By 1989, more than 25 agencies and organizations had lent their technical and financial support to the initiative. In 1990, the Central American Presidents reaffirmed 'the conviction that the health of the Central American peoples is a political priority that requires the preservation and strengthening of joint actions aimed at improving health conditions, and which are intended to be a bridge for peace and understanding in the area'. The second phase of the plan, 'Health and Peace for Development and Democracy' served as a major social development initiative specifically designed to parallel and support the Esquipulas Peace Process.

In May 1995, the World Health Assembly requested the Director-General, *inter alia*, 'to strengthen WHO's advocacy for the respect and protection of health personnel and infrastructure in conflict situations, in accordance with the concept of health as an investment for peace' (Res. WHA48.2).

The WHO Division of Emergency and Humanitarian Action then initiated the Health as a Bridge for Peace Project to study this concept, in order to better integrate advocacy for peace through health into EHA functions and to develop practical guidance on peacebuilding skills for health professionals.

Health professionals may have a special role to play in peacekeeping on account of their humane and humanitarian calling, their professional codes of ethics that impose fundamental obligations on physicians and nurses, their respect for human life and dignity, their professional skills, and their neutrality and impartiality regarding victims in armed conflicts. Among professionals in all fields, they enjoy high social and professional legitimacy and respect. The role of the health professional as the 'healer' and their intimate relationship with individuals and communities may open doors in other sectors. The expectation is that health may be considered by political and military leaders and populations as a super-ordinate goal in pre-conflict, conflict and post-conflict situations. Friends and foes may be brought together by sharing, and acting on, common health values.

WHO's commitment for public health, development and peace should place its representatives in a key position to promote dialogue and joint action in health matters within the overall peace process, in conflict prevention, conflict reduction and rehabilitation.

WHO should provide guidance to health professionals on their roles and responsibilities in situations of real or potential conflict. WHO and health professionals could play a role in creating an environment conducive to bringing together opposing parties, for example, by identifying an area of common interest and concern, such as water supply, disease control and children's immunization. In some situations, health could serve as an entry point to 'proximity talks' or could facilitate a rapprochement between groups in conflict.

The 1996 Consultation

In a first consultation convened by WHO in Geneva on 'Health as a Bridge for Peace', a number of conclusions and recommendations were adopted.[8] Among these were:

- WHO's particular strengths include strict neutrality and impartiality, which facilitates its honest-broker role in conflict situations. Its established physical presence in almost all countries enables it to provide up-to-date information and assessment in conflict situations;
- Prior to the outbreak of potential conflicts, WHO should document and provide projections on such parameters as mortality, high-survivor morbidity, potential demographic consequences, mental trauma,

collapse of social support systems, long-term adjustment problems (notably physical and mental), and intergenerational problems, as well as the anticipated cost – in both financial and institutional terms – of potential conflicts;

- WHO should provide a neutral forum for initiating dialogue between otherwise irreconcilable parties even before the outbreak of conflict – dialogue that can thereafter continue in other fora;
- WHO should intensify its role of neutral broker during periods of war with relevant partners, such as national professional health associations and organizations;
- Review modalities for excluding health from conflicts;
- Develop and promote a public health and epidemiological approach to the study of inhumane weapons, such as landmines or biological weapons, as pathological agents affecting human health in order to define the right approaches to therapy and control;
- Promote the establishment of 'WHO-protected' hospitals whose neutrality would be respected by all parties in situations of conflict;
- Equip the health sector with preparedness mechanisms for dealing with potential conflicts;
- Promote the training of health professionals to respect codes of ethics requiring the medical treatment of all patients, irrespective of status.

The Annecy Meeting – 1997

A Consultative Meeting was convened by WHO in Annecy, 30–31 October 1997, as part of the Health as a Bridge for Peace project, sponsored by the Department of International Development of the UK. The main purpose of the project is to develop practical guidance on peacebuilding skills for health professionals. Its report gave useful and critical assessments of the potential and limits of the HBP concept. On the basis of documented experiences, the following courses of action were identified:

- 'At the latent phase, health for peace actions include the promotion of Health for All, working towards human development in order to address inequities that exacerbate conflict and violence, and advocating for the abolition or limited use of weapons with unacceptable health effects, such as nuclear weapons and landmines.
- During the stage of violent conflict, health professionals, and WHO in particular, may contribute to the promotion of health and peace by providing opportunities for dialogue between conflicting sides through joint cooperation in health, the coordination of health and humanitarian responses, and the preservation and protection of the health of civilian populations.

• During the stage of rehabilitation, there seems to be an opportunity to act as a neutral broker to bring conflicting sides together in joint health activities, to aid in activities such as the demobilization of troops, and to participate in guiding strategies for reconstruction and development that have health as a key component.'

In all stages of conflict, the group agreed that reliable health data could be a powerful and convincing tool to move public opinion and instigate policy change.

The meeting wisely noted that health cannot be a substitute for political action, but it can monitor the political evolution of the peace process and take advantage of situations in which it can operate to reinforce the peacebuilding efforts. It emphasized that the understanding of humanitarian and human rights law by health professionals is essential in conflict environments. Furthermore, health professionals, including WHO staff, should have or acquire certain skills in order to work in health/peace initiatives, including:

• understanding of and sensitivity to the political, legal, socio-economic environment of the country;
• capacity to identify opportunities and crucial issues to bring technical people from conflicting parties to meet and work together;
• leadership, mediating, problem solving skills;
• proposing clear technical principles as a basis for negotiations to avoid political manipulation of aid.

Finally, the meeting identified the specific role that WHO can play in promoting peace:

• to act as a facilitator, or a catalyst to bring health professionals from all sides together on technical issues of common interest;
• to set standards of 'best practices' in public health aimed at reducing conflict and promoting reconciliation;
• to network with other professional institutions and individuals in supporting peacebuilding and violence reduction initiatives;
• to coordinate with other UN agencies, international organizations and NGOs in implementing peace processes in the health sector.

The group recommended that HBP be placed within the policy framework of WHO, through the Renewal of Health for All process, and that the HBP effort be housed in WHO/EHA.

Conclusion

There is a clear connection between health and peace: the development of public health needs peace, as does economic and social development in general. War destroys lives, causes physical and mental damage among both the military and civilians, damages or destroys health institutions and infrastructure, disrupts health services, arouses ethnic, religious or other hatreds, uses financial resources for destruction. It is also true that health professionals enjoy a particular prestige due to their humane vocation, healing and technical skills, closeness to individuals and communities. However, health professionals are not in the commanding position of political and military leaders. Their functions are to promote health, care and cure in peace and war, to attempt to deliver health services during conflicts, to care for all victims impartially and without consideration of sex, race, nationality, religion, political affiliation or any other criteria. Unless they have been elected or appointed to leadership positions, their responsibilities are limited to specialized, sectoral activities.

In any government, ministries of health are generally ancillary to such 'powerful' ministries as departments of war or defence, foreign affairs, domestic affairs or the economy. Health ministers may, at best, exert a secondary influence on major political decisions, such as war and peace.

Excluding health from conflicts is desirable but unrealistic: external and civil wars exacerbate passions which override most humanitarian attempts to set limits to war abuses and excesses. Deep-seated roots of conflict are well beyond the reach of medical care.

WHO is not a supranational organization: it has no powers over governments and other organizations, although it may exert influence acquired through its own technical competence and its achievements, its universal presence, its capacity to call on the best experts in all health fields for advice. However, its mandate is sectoral. It does not include a general peacemaking function as such, although its work may contribute to peacebuilding.

Can Health for All create or restore peace? The original objective of Health for All was the attainment by the year 2000 by all the people in the world of a level of health that would permit them to lead a socially and economically productive life, a mandate now under review and a target being extended. Its purpose is not to prevent or stop wars, nor to build peace. If its objective is achieved in specific countries, there is no evidence that healthy people will refrain from engaging in wars and atrocities. There is no evidence either that poor populations with inadequate health protection will be more or less bellicose than rich and healthy ones. Health for All has defined a useful and worthy social target for governments and

WHO, whether or not it contributes to peace.

Within the UN system, the organization in charge of peace and security is the UN itself, not WHO. The Security Council, the General Assembly, the UN Secretary-General have a central and direct responsibility in preventive diplomacy, peacemaking, peacekeeping and peacebuilding. The experience gained so far by WHO shows that it has had no role in preventing conflicts, a limited role during conflicts, but that it has played a useful, sectoral role in peacebuilding following a conflict. Neither the UN nor WHO have had any effective role in preventing the conflict in Former Yugoslavia or the Rwandan genocide. Truces negotiated with parties in conflict for immunization have benefitted children in a number of countries, but there is no evidence that these lead to firm ceasefires, peace settlements and reconciliation. Humanitarian protection of health personnel and non-combatants during conflicts is a responsibility of the ICRC, not WHO. Creating WHO-protected hospitals is not desirable: hospitals are or should be protected by the ICRC under the Geneva Conventions. The failure of the UN-protected 'safe-havens' in former Yugoslavia is another reason for WHO to abstain from such an unrealistic venture.

WHO operations related to peacemaking have usually been part of broader political peace programmes initiated by governments, the UN and other organizations: they were not separate, independent initiatives. For instance, the WHO/PAHO 'Health as a Bridge to Peace' initiative stemmed from negotiations in the Contadora Group, then from the Esquipulas peace plan broached by the five Central American presidents in 1987, with support from the UN and the OAS. UNICEF, UNFPA, UNDP, a number of governments and the European Community (now Union) and NGOs, participated in the initiative.

WHO's confidence-building efforts in Eastern Slavonia, aimed at implementing joint health activities between Croatian and Serbian health professionals, were carried out not independently, but within the framework established by the UN Transitional Administration and in cooperation with UNHCR. WHO's health programmes in Angola were one element in the long-term UN effort to help the government and UNITA achieve reconciliation and restore peace in the country.

Health data may be used effectively to demonstrate that certain weapons have unacceptable and inhumane effects. The ICRC and other NGOs have used reliable epidemiological data and images in their landmine campaign, as a basis to convince policy-makers and public opinion. International Physicians for the Prevention of Nuclear War have used data and advocacy to promote the adoption of the atmospheric test ban treaty.

Should WHO contribute to such campaigns and intervene as an organization? WHO maintains its technical role, that of initiating research, developing and disseminating reliable health and epidemiological data on the effects of the use of such weapons on the population. However, WHO's experience with the World Court has shown that the organization should remain within its technical mandate, and not launch campaigns which may open it to charges of politicization. These campaigns should be left to NGOs, whose freedom of expression and action make them more effective than an IGO.

Peacebuilding in the health field following a conflict is a legitimate part of WHO's mandate. It may include physical and functional rehabilitation of health institutions, joint training of health professionals from former enemy camps, specific physical and mental rehabilitation programmes for victims and survivors.

As noted by the Annecy group, health cannot be a substitute for political action. However, WHO can reinforce peacebuilding efforts in identifying health areas for its intervention, in close cooperation with other UN agencies, other IGOs, government agencies and NGOs. Whether WHO can direct these efforts depends on its own prestige, proven capacity and leadership, and on the acceptance of other organizations that WHO should be appointed as lead agency for a specific programme. HBP should be included within the policy framework of WHO/EHA, with due account being taken of the limits of the concept and of its application.

In conclusion, health must remain WHO's central objective. Support for peace can only be a desirable, worthy but complementary and occasional activity for the organization, within its limited resources.

ACKNOWLEDGEMENTS

The views expressed in this contribution are those of the author and do not necessarily represent the views of the World Health Organization or other organizations referred to. All documents refer to WHO documents unless otherwise identified.

NOTES

1. Doc. WHA45/1992/REC/2, 5 May 1992.
2. Doc. A49/27, 25 March 1996; Jean-Paul Menu, 'A New Role for WHO in Emergencies', *World Health Statistical Quarterly*, Vol.49, 1996, p.169.
3. 'Emergency and Humanitarian Action, 1996 Activities', 1997, p.25. (Referred to below as 'EHA-1996').
4. Press Release, WHO/34, 25 April 1996.
5. Press Release WHO/63, 24 September 1995; 'EHA-1996', p.12.
6. WHO Fact Sheet No.90, July 1995, 'EHA-1996', pp.16–17; Press Release WHO/51, 26 June 1997. WHO and UNICEF have also brokered ceasefires and truces to allow polio immunization campaigns to be conducted in El Salvador, Lebanon, Uganda, Sudan and the Philippines.

7. Hedip's steering committee includes UN/DHA, the International Federation of Red Cross and Red Crescent Societies, ILO, UNDP, UNICEF, UNHCR, WFP, WHO and WWF. Hedip is managed by WHO and financed by the Italian government. See *Hedip Forum*, Nos 1–4, 1994.
8. Doc. WHO/HPD/96.7 Rev.1, 'Report of the consultation on Health as a Bridge for Peace', Geneva, 1996.

Civilian–Military Interactions and Ongoing UN Reforms: DHA's Past and OCHA's Remaining Challenges

THOMAS G. WEISS

The pragmatic and visionary options for the creation of a successor to the UN Department of Humanitarian Affairs are outlined, together with the political and bureaucratic considerations which led instead to the establishment of the Office for the Coordination of Humanitarian Affairs, which falls short of what was possible as well as desirable. In order to appreciate the forces which are likely to converge on OCHA, a history of the formation and performance of DHA is detailed, followed by an examination of the prospects for OCHA in meeting its three stated core functions: policy development, advocacy and coordination. Despite a number of improvements over the form and standing of its predecessor, OCHA's prospects for success are constrained by the nature and extent of the UN reform process, the operational realities of humanitarian operations, a variety of unaddressed institutional inadequacies and entrenched resistance to coordination.

The central challenge for civilian humanitarians in tandem with outside military forces – be they traditional peacekeepers[1] or more robust peace-enforcers[2] – remains the same now as in 1991: how can the UN system, along with a host of non-governmental organizations including many serving as subcontractors,[3] function cohesively rather than as a loose collection of independent actors with separate mandates, budgets, fundraising arrangements, priorities and programmes? The establishment of the UN's Department of Humanitarian Affairs in April 1992 – the same month that the European Community established its Humanitarian Office – was a response to the palpable frustrations of major donors with the inability of multiple UN agencies and loosely associated NGOs to coordinate effectively their activities in the Gulf. DHA was replaced in January 1998 by the Office for the Coordination of Humanitarian Affairs.[4] The challenges facing this office are formidable in spite of and perhaps because of Secretary-General Kofi Annan's reform package of July 1997,[5] which was developed under the supervision of Maurice Strong, special advisor in the role of Executive Coordinator for United Nations Reform.

Thomas G. Weiss, Distinguished Professor of Political Science, The Graduate School and University Center, The City University of New York.

The creation of DHA in 1992 was an explicit recognition of unacceptable fumbling by humanitarian agencies and of the crying need to orchestrate better civilian inputs. As the decade proceeded, the awkward interface between military and humanitarian elements became something of an obsession in such theatres as the Gulf, the Balkans, Somalia, Rwanda, and Haiti. No one was pleased with DHA's impact on operations, and few regretted its departure, which had figured prominently in early discussions about institutional changes by then newly-elected Secretary-General Annan. But the requirement to improve civilian–military interactions remains as does the demonstrated lack of political and bureaucratic will to create an effective institutional structure – in short, to replace rhetoric with an operational reality.

The author participated in an independent assessment of UN humanitarian action in the Gulf crises, which contained one of the first calls for a DHA-like structure to foster 'the systematic utilization of policy instruments to deliver humanitarian assistance in a cohesive and systematic manner'.[6] Over half a decade later and in spite of several new crises as laboratories, effective coordination of civilian–military interactions is still required for: strategic planning; gathering data and managing information; resource mobilization; procedures to enhance accountability and professionalism; the orchestration of a better division of labour in the field; negotiations with host authorities; and leadership.

The most obvious – although politically and bureaucratically the least feasible – way to foster such coordination would be more centralization, with independent and often dysfunctional intergovernmental and non-governmental agencies setting aside rivalries and ceding autonomy. Otherwise, so-called UN restructuring will continue incessantly and be accompanied by the familiar charade that a pluricentral non-system can be made to function as if it were a centrally-organized system.

Humanitarian action unites rather than divides peoples, parliaments and administrations. There is more support for change here than in other sectors. Unfortunately, minimal changes in humanitarian mechanisms do not bode well for structural reforms elsewhere in the UN system. Civilian–military interactions were not the only or even the main reason behind DHA's creation. But they have been and will remain central to international responses in the most severe war-induced emergencies; and hence they will also remain challenges facing the OCHA.[7] These interactions provide the focus for this essay and the justification for its inclusion in this collection.

This essay explores the so-called reform of 1997 and the DHA's five-year track record with a view towards making suggestions about improving OCHA's impact. Readers will appreciate the operational and political implications for blue helmets under Chapter VI or Chapter VII of the UN Charter.

The Aborted Reform of 1997

Two dramatic options for structural changes – one pragmatic, and one more visionary – had been under active consideration when predictable organizational defensiveness kicked in and resulted in a 'shell game' rather than any significant reform.[8] Although dismissed by many observers as the playthings of bureaucrats, UN reforms or lack thereof have direct operational repercussions for the secretariat's ability to respond to crises. It thus is worth examining those options that were set aside as a prelude to what remains to be done. The modified system falls considerably short of alternatives that had previously been at least pondered seriously.

One late draft had recommended that the office of the UN High Commissioner for Refugees be asked to assume DHA's functions. In effect UNHCR would have been in the driver's seat for the international humanitarian system – becoming the 'permanent lead agency' for assistance to war victims in addition to exercising its traditional protection responsibilities for refugees. This recommendation would have amounted to a pragmatic adaptation of UNHCR's efforts to illuminate the Balkan gloom, where it embraced the challenge of displacement and cared for refugees, returnees, internally displaced persons, and those who had not moved at all.[9] Ironically, the Secretary-General praised UNHCR's pragmatic performance in the former Yugoslavia (para. 192), but ultimately he did not act on this insight.

The orchestration and management of the various inputs and programmes of the UN system – the military, political, humanitarian and human rights dimensions – is extraordinarily complicated. It is not for nothing that the label 'complex emergency' has gained currency. And orchestration does not become easier when economic and social inputs are infused in a post-war phase. A clear chain of command is required in war zones, where the entire system and the largest international NGOs working as subcontractors could and should constitute a coherent and effective response mechanism. Rather than extant feudal arrangements, a single body is necessary to set priorities, to raise and distribute resources, and to coordinate emergency inputs.

This seemingly obvious – but politically and bureaucratically problematic – consolidation of the UN presence has been recommended by this author[10] and a variation by former WFP Executive Director James Ingram in the form of a revamped International Committee of the Red Cross.[11] Disparate views of course remain among Western governments about the exact shape of such a mechanism. Moreover, their bilateral aid agencies themselves are not more efficient and sincere – in fact, often the call from governments for 'UN coordination' is duplicitous in light of the collective and individual unwillingness to do less national flag-waving in tragedies.

Centralization moves in and out of mainstream intergovernmental discussions depending on the existence of a world-class crisis. For instance, former US Secretary of State Warren Christopher's 'non-paper' at the July 1995 session of the Economic and Social Council proposed considering 'whether and how to consolidate the emergency functions of the UN High Commissioner for Refugees (UNHCR), the World Food Programme (WFP), the UN Children's Fund (UNICEF), and the Department of Humanitarian Affairs (DHA) into a single agency'.[12] These views are not Washington's alone. For example, Jan Pronk, the Dutch Minister for Development Cooperation, stated at the 1996 General Assembly: 'At the field level, integration and efficiency for the sake of comprehensive conflict prevention could be enhanced if there would be only one UN-representative in a country, representing the entire UN-system, including the specialized agencies.'[13]

Christopher's and Pronk's views about consolidation reflected the trauma of Rwanda. Albeit still controversial, centralization emerged from the unprecedented multinational, multi-donor evaluation of the international response to the Rwandan tragedy;[14] but it evaporated from the international agenda because there was no Rwanda-like crisis in 1996, 1997 or 1998. However, the need for a consolidated UN presence in war zones is bound to reappear on the international agenda when Burundi or the Congo or Kosovo explodes. Some officials are still quietly pushing the issue, which would, in fact, build upon a host of earlier proposals by seasoned practitioners.[15]

In spite of the compelling logic, consolidating the UN's emergency capabilities within a new institution appeared too visionary an option in earlier drafts of the Secretary-General's report. However, it was at least to have appeared as an annex. The implication was that this more imaginative option was politically and bureaucratically infeasible but *not* undesirable. Moreover, unlike the transfer of responsibilities to UNHCR, the establishment of a centralized structure would have had substantial legal hurdles because it would have necessitated constitutional decisions by member states.

The General Assembly acted upon a final report containing neither the proposal to rely upon UNHCR (the pragmatic option) nor reference to a unitary humanitarian agency (the visionary option). Rather, it proposed the continuation of the status quo with cosmetic changes – hard to fathom in light of endless complaints from donor governments and recipients as well as the bulk of officials from partners in intergovernmental and non-governmental organizations. The feasible proposal was overturned by the public and private stances by the heads of the other two most important UN players – UNICEF and WFP – and of American NGOs through the voice of their consortium, InterAction. The vision of a consolidated international humanitarian system appeared so pollyannaish that it had been deleted altogether.

The disappearance of the practical option from the Strong document is worth reviewing because of the implications for any substantial changes in how the UN system conducts its business. UNICEF's senior management apparently had second thoughts about the implications for its 'brand name' and ability to raise funds, privately and from governments, that were likely to result from UNHCR's assumption of such a visible role in leading the UN charge in complex emergencies. With 80 per cent of its $1 billion annual budget resulting from emergency food relief, WFP's reluctance to support unequivocally a rival agency to be permanently in charge of complex emergencies is easy to understand in purely financial terms. After having supported major structural changes, NGOs apparently came to fear that the Strong option went too far in marginalizing DHA. Having been one of the primary beneficiaries of DHA's opening towards NGOs, the Washington-based consortium was seemingly distressed by the looming relocation of the coordination nexus to Geneva and away from New York.

Some observers argued that UNHCR had overplayed its hand in going public with plans for implementing a new arrangement. The assumption of a tactical error minimizes two essential arguments relating to UNHCR's bureaucratic interests in resisting change and to the merits of a strong lead agency. Substantial numbers of officials in UNHCR were against the change, arguing that the organization should emphasize protection, not assistance; and the expansion of its operational role would have *de facto* diluted protection.[16] The massive expansion first in the former Yugoslavia and then in the African Great Lakes had contributed to an institutional overstretch that meant 'it has lost its soul',[17] and to the need to consider modifying principles as part of 'instrumental humanitarianism'.[18] More important, Strong had requested UNHCR Commissioner Sadako Ogata – not vice versa – to prepare a background note on implementation. Perhaps he had overstepped his mandate. In any event, his request was imprudent because subsequently the Secretary-General back-peddled and argued that he himself had made no firm decision to put UNHCR in the driver's seat.

The final document thus proposed and the General Assembly approved reducing the numbers of DHA staff but leaving intact a poorly positioned and poorly functioning unit. In order to understand the Sisyphean challenges faced by OCHA, it would be worth revisiting why DHA was established in the first place and what it actually did from 1992 to 1997.

The Creation of DHA

As mentioned earlier, the disappointing performance of the international humanitarian system in 'groping and coping in the Gulf crisis'[19] led to the call for a new coordination mechanism to help overcome the shortcomings resulting from the lack of cohesion among civilian humanitarian agencies. The Secretary-General specifies this historical catalyst for the establishment of DHA in *Renewing the United Nations* (para. 183). The Office of the UN Disaster Relief Coordinator had been founded in 1971 in order to focus essentially on natural disasters,[20] and it was incorporated into the new department.

But the DHA's real purpose was to improve international responses to the massive suffering from the growing number of man-made disasters of the 1990s. Although civilian–military interactions were a relatively minor area of DHA's mandate, all the major complex emergencies of the 1990s witnessed the use of outside military forces and personnel. Necessarily then, the implication for coordination of such interactions became more pertinent. And DHA's Military–Civilian Disaster Unit increasingly moved beyond the logistics for natural disasters that had been the focus of UNDRO's Military and Civil Defence Assets. Thus, MCDU became involved in thinking about the use of the military in war-induced catastrophes as well, which was relevant particularly in DHA's internal relations with the other two main UN departments, peace-keeping operations (DPKO) and political affairs (DPA). Founded to work out logistical stand-by arrangements with national militaries for use in natural disasters, the MCDU evolved as a tool more broadly available to DHA and potentially the system as a whole.

International, and particularly Western, reactions to tragedies in the last half decade have unleashed humanitarian impulses. Whether or not we actually are in Raimo Väyrynen's 'age of humanitarian emergencies',[21] ensuring better access to and treatment of victims clearly preoccupies policymakers, pundits, parliamentarians and publics. UN peace operations have been in the vanguard, and most have had humanitarian dimensions. In a recent review of literature published between 1989 and 1996, about one-quarter of the 2,200 entries related to outside military forces under UN auspices in complex emergencies of the post-Cold War period.[22]

The more routine involvement by third party military forces in humanitarian efforts in war zones is striking, but the use of armed forces for such purposes is hardly new.[23] There is often an automatic association, particularly in the Western public's mind, between the military and disaster relief. The expectation is that the armed forces will assist civilian populations after an emergency strikes. In the last decade, virtually all Western militaries have sponsored proposals and conferences. 'Operations other than war' (OOTW) is the preferred term at the Pentagon and is acceptable to other militaries.[24] The integration of political, military, and humanitarian missions, or 'peace-maintenance', is a striking conceptual change from earlier and more specialized analyses of peacekeeping.[25] As one observer remarked about the American military, but with more general applicability: 'For the near future our military is more likely to participate in humanitarian interventions and in peacekeeping than it is to participate in war or in peace enforcement.'[26]

The civilian humanitarian partners of UN blue helmets have become more numerous and their relationships more complex and controversial than before the end of the Cold War.[27] However, Adam Roberts has aptly identified the 'vacuum'[28] in thinking about security relationships as humanitarian responses have become more politicized, more militarized, and more intra-state than their predecessors. Consequently, enhanced coordination is increasingly viewed as essential, not only to orchestrate complex institutional inputs but also to situate them in relation to political and military factors and actors. The resort to outside military forces under UN command or auspices has complicated and often exacerbated long-standing problems about the lack of cohesion in the UN's civilian humanitarian inputs. The number of peace operations has declined from the mid-1990s peak. Although many believe that the future is more likely to witness traditional peacekeeping rather than enforcement,[29] the issue of military–civilian interactions remains and undoubtedly will reappear in the years to come. If for no other reason than the increasing reluctance of rich and poor countries alike to admit asylum-seekers or refugees,[30] international responses will continue to focus on countries of origin. The possibilities for military involvement will then combine to colour discourse.

An obvious path to improved international responses leads to a better division of labour among the various political and military parts of the UN family and its most important operational humanitarian partners – essentially UNHCR, WFP and UNICEF. In December 1991, on the heels of the clumsy efforts in the Gulf, General Assembly resolution 46/182 called for an Emergency Relief Coordinator, in essence to harmonize the diplomacy and especially the implementation of UN humanitarian efforts. In April 1992, then newly-elected Secretary-General Boutros Boutros-Ghali gave an important boost to the concept by allocating an Under-Secretary-General post to the new Department of Humanitarian Affairs.[31]

Jan Eliasson, the able Swedish ambassador in New York who had helped to negotiate the end to the Iran–Iraq War in 1987 and to shepherd the controversial resolution 46/182[32] through the General Assembly, became the first occupant to the new post. As a national from an important donor state at the head of a department that responded to donor dissatisfactions,

Eliasson logically pursued four tasks seen as crucial by governments that were financing so much of the growing bill for international responses to complex emergencies: to gather and manage information; define, prioritize and consolidate requirements for donors; negotiate inter-agency frameworks for action and orchestrate field activities; and provide leadership.[33] However, he sorely lacked the necessary management experience to run a major UN department in a complicated area of responsibility. If someone had been found who met the basic requirements for the post as called for by Brian Urquhart and Erskine Childers,[34] DHA might have been a different story. For example, the Office of Emergency Operations in Africa had been a success story in the 1980s largely because the managerial knowledge and political savvy of Bradford Morse and Maurice Strong were powerful enough to break or bend UN institutional rules and practices, just as Sir Robert Jackson had done in the Bangladesh emergency in 1971. Under Mrs. Sadako Ogata's leadership since 1991, UNHCR has become recognized by donor governments as an accomplished rule-breaker akin to the earlier but transient predecessors, Morse and Strong and Jackson.

Behind the mask of public eloquence was basic management ineptitude. Not to put too fine a point on it, the DHA had insufficient qualified staff, resources and authority to become a permanent rule-breaker. Under Eliasson, as well as his successors – Peter Hansen, a respected Danish development economist with lengthy UN experience, and Yasushi Akashi, who had held a number of senior UN posts in New York and in peace operations in Cambodia and the former Yugoslavia – the DHA made little practical difference during almost six years of existence. Nor was it successful in internal lobbying on humanitarian issues with the last Secretary-General and his cabinet and with the Security Council.

DHA's Role, 1992–97

'Perhaps the greatest difficulty confronting the DHA,' Gil Loescher wrote in 1997, 'is that the specialized agencies, including the UNHCR, have a high degree of constitutional autonomy and independence and have resisted any attempt by the DHA to impose strong authority.'[35] Within the UN system, the Secretary-General is *primus inter pares* (first among equals). But the emphasis is on the latter half of the expression. The executive heads of UNHCR, WFP and UNICEF, as well as the UN Development Programme, each manage annual budgets that approach the resources of the UN regular budget over which the Secretary-General himself has direct control. What was particularly unrealistic was any expectation that an Under-Secretary-General at the helm of DHA – that is, with inferior rank and resources – could be expected to knock heads together and coordinate more senior officials who controlled vastly superior human and financial resources. Andrew Natsios noted with respect to the UN's four major humanitarian organizations that 'Perhaps the one matter on which they are united is constraining DHA.'[36] Autonomy, not integration and collaboration, are the hallmarks of this feudal system, whether the subject matter is humanitarian relief or international peace and security, human rights or sustainable development.[37]

How exactly were these structural shortcomings manifest during the course of DHA's existence?[38] Information management is important and non-threatening. And in terms of gathering and managing information, DHA was helpful in mounting assessment missions, particularly in actively seeking out and integrating NGO perspectives into the mainstream of intergovernmental debate and action. The information-sharing system within genocide-plagued Rwanda in 1994, for example, was valued even by critical observers.[39] Moreover, the construction and maintenance of the Relief Web was also viewed by many practitioners as a service to the international humanitarian system as was the establishment of two units for West and East Africa of the Integrated Regional Information Network (IRIN).

In terms of resource mobilization for the complex emergencies of this decade, UN consolidated appeals were conducted by DHA but represented little by way of value-added. Setting aside for a moment the accuracy of assessments, responses by donor governments to joint appeals have been disappointing, with only about two-thirds of estimated needs actually mobilized in 1995 and 1996.[40] Such shortfalls were not exclusively the responsibility of DHA but mainly of UN member states. However, the unit can be criticized because its 'packaging' was tied to headquarters rather than field perspectives, and because NGO requests usually receive less attention than those from UN counterparts. In order to respect organizational perspectives and autarchy, these appeals have constituted more a 'shopping list' of individual requests from UN agencies rather than a meaningful consolidation with professional judgements about sequencing and relative importance.[41] The acute need remains to define, prioritize, and consolidate intergovernmental and non-governmental requirements for donor consideration.

In terms of negotiating inter-agency frameworks for action and orchestrating field activities – the key element behind its establishment – DHA's efforts were discouraging at best. The Inter-Agency Standing Committee, on paper, is a significant breakthrough in bringing together with staff support from DHA the central representatives of the entire international humanitarian system – including the main UN organizations, the Red Cross movement, and major international NGO coordination bodies. But this mechanism was unable to remain small and businesslike in order to accommodate the dominant centrifugal forces of the UN system. This would have required more than moral suasion and common sense but vision and support at the highest political and administrative levels.

In the field DHA attempted a host of experiments after April 1992, but DHA's lack of leverage, paucity of seasoned personnel, and absence of control over resources other than an inadequate ($50 million) Central Emergency Revolving Fund[42] added a layer of bureaucracy rather than added value.[43] As mentioned earlier, the need for enhanced collaboration was pushed by donors who saw that the international system increasingly confronted a new type of tragedy for which responses by civilian humanitarian organizations systematically took place side-by-side with military operations under UN auspices. These interactions reinforced the perceived need for coordination, the logic being that less waste and more impact was especially compelling when huge numbers of lives were menaced.

Antonio Donini makes useful distinctions among three broad categories of coordination within the United Nations:

*   Coordination by command: coordination in which strong leadership is accompanied by some sort of authority, whether carrot or stick;
*   Coordination by consensus: coordination in which leadership is essentially a function of the capacity to orchestrate a coherent response and to mobilize the key actors around common objectives and priorities. Consensus in this instance is normally achieved without any direct assertion of authority by the coordinator;
*   Coordination by default: coordination that, in the absence of a formal coordination entity, involves only the most rudimentary exchange of information and division of labour among the actors.[44]

These distinctions should be viewed not as air-tight categories, but rather as points on a spectrum. Given the sacrosanct autonomy of organizational components within the UN system, coordination by command is clearly unrealistic, however desirable, particularly in the context of coercive military operations. The experience of DHA under the best of circumstances – for instance, during the first six months after the Rwandan genocide – could undoubtedly be described as coordination by consensus. Under the worst of circumstances – for instance, in the chaos of Liberia – coordination was largely absent, and what did exist could be labelled as coordination by default.

In the absence of meaningful central authority – or 'coordination light'[45] rued by proponents of centralization – some critics and practitioners argue that all UN coordination mechanisms constitute a hindrance rather than a help. Extreme proponents of laissez-faire humanitarian action argue that a coherent strategy is unwise because it works against the magic of the marketplace in which individual agencies pursue independent strategies and arrive at a sound division of labour. A subtler view is that creative chaos is better than botched efforts at coherence, which is all that is possible within the UN system. The process is better self-regulated than poorly coordinated because one less layer of bureaucracy rather than one more is preferable. As no one is really in charge and no one can be sure what will work, so the argument goes, why not make the best of it rather than merely adding a ceremonial layer of a DHA or an OCHA?

In terms of providing leadership within the UN's front office, humanitarian perspectives appeared to finish continually in third place behind the considerations of DPKO and DPA. Part of the explanation, according to many staff within the secretariat, was the low priority – some would even claim disinterest – accorded to humanitarian issues by former Secretary-General Boutros-Ghali. In any event, what Eliasson had dubbed 'humanitarian diplomacy' was certainly not given equal billing in New York throughout the tenure of the last Secretary-General. This imbalance and absence of meaningful coordination were precisely the *raison d'être* behind the establishment of DHA in the first place. It is too early to tell whether this imbalance has changed dramatically under the present Secretary-General especially because there have as yet been no new major peace operations in complex emergencies.

Challenges for OCHA

The reform package breaks little new ground and certainly not enough to justify what a hyperbolic UN press release in July 1997 boasted was 'the most extensive and far-reaching reform of the United Nations since it was founded 52 years ago'.[46] One senior official close to the process summarized its contents as 'having hatched a mouse', and in no arena is this summary more apt than for humanitarian affairs. In an understatement, the Secretary-General concludes (para. 76) that 'It is also clear that improvements are necessary in the coordination and rapid deployment of United Nations' humanitarian responses' – a performance that he would later more straightforwardly describe as 'problematic'.[47]

For the OCHA, the report emphasizes and the General Assembly subsequently approved 'three core functions: (1) policy development, (2) advocacy of humanitarian issues with political organizations, notably the Security Council, and (3) coordination of humanitarian emergency response, by ensuring that an appropriate response mechanism is established, through IASC consultations, on the ground' (para. 186). What is the likelihood that the OCHA can rise to meet these three challenges?

Policy Development

The inability of any intergovernmental unit to undertake independent policy work is obvious to those who have tried to navigate the shoals of basic UN research efforts. The constraints result from governments' looking over shoulders of senior administrators as well as self-imposed censorship from staff who do not wish to run risks. Original ideas and hard-hitting criticism of business-as-usual are far more likely to emanate from universities, think tanks and NGO policy units than from the United Nations. The OCHA has no comparative advantage in relation to independent analysts.

Less penetrating, but necessary, examinations of how UN institutions themselves have fared or could organize themselves provide more fertile ground. Perhaps the best example of what might be done were the efforts to develop an inter-agency dialogue about 'humanitarian mandates'. Despite foot-dragging by other members of the IASC and especially by DPKO and DPA, the history of this three-year effort provides a kind of example for OCHA's future policy work. So too would be more open and honest efforts to 'learn lessons' from operational problems. This term has entered international parlance, and there are multiple units with related titles within the UN system – this in itself being an illustration of how few lessons have been learned. To qualify as 'learning', action must be taken to alter previous modes of behaviour and to institutionalize them, not merely to identify problems and diagnose likely causes. There is considerable room for the OCHA to take the lead and improve upon evaluations across agencies, to ensure that lessons are 'learned' as opposed to being 'compiled' in filing cabinets.

It would also be useful for the Secretary-General to have better informed views about fluid humanitarian subjects likely to require inter-agency perspectives and action. For instance, was it wise to keep the old DHA out of the human rights field in light of the horrors of Rwanda? What types of cooperation and 'mainstreaming' of human rights, in the field and in New York and Geneva, are most compelling with the new consolidated unit under the direction of High Commissioner for Human Rights, Mary Robinson? Or what was learned from DHA's earlier and marginal involvement in demining and reconstruction now that the OCHA is being asked to concentrate only on emergency relief? This type of informed counsel about institutional priorities and practices would be a possible focus for the OCHA, a kind of NSC for humanitarian issues.

Advocacy

'Limited leverage' would perhaps be the most that could be said of the possibility of the OCHA's substantially influencing Security Council decisions. As former Under-Secretary-General Akashi stated: 'Sometimes it is very difficult to find humanitarian space...even in New York.'[48] It should be more feasible, however, to ensure that humanitarian perspectives are better integrated into the deliberations on the 38th floor of the UN secretariat than they were under the last Secretary-General. As such, perhaps some lessons could be gleaned from informal briefings in 1997 that were arranged for the Security Council regarding the African Great Lakes and sanctions. Although this is perhaps low-key advocacy, it nonetheless appears useful in terms of getting humanitarian perspectives more squarely in front of the council's members.

In February 1997 at the suggestion of then Chilean Ambassador Juan Somavia (who has subsequently become the Director-General of the International Labour Organization), who had been pushing for the inclusion of humanitarian perspectives, CARE, Oxfam and Médecins Sans Frontières met with the members of the Security Council to discuss the crisis in the Great Lakes Region of Eastern Africa. This built upon the precedent set earlier by which the president of the Security Council meets monthly with the New York delegate of the ICRC. In June 1997, a group of researchers – again at the behest of Somavia – placed their draft conclusions about the humanitarian impacts of economic sanctions before a private meeting of the 15 member states.[49]

These sessions have begun to penetrate the state monopoly on humanitarian perspectives even within Security Council chambers. Building upon such precedents should be high on the OCHA agenda, which would require constant efforts to establish and maintain links with knowledgeable and independent researchers. It also would necessitate running the risks of having privileged relations with respected NGOs and policy analysts rather than being politically correct and embracing or rejecting all agencies without discrimination.

Coordination

The third core OCHA function identified by the Secretary-General and decided upon by the General Assembly influences directly the effectiveness of peace operations. It is also exactly the same main shortcoming that had motivated the previous humanitarian reform in 1992. In moving beyond 'blue-speak' and examining the likely impact of the actions specified in paragraph 191 of *Renewing the United Nations*, two functions of the old DHA have quite sensibly been reassigned to UNDP (for natural disaster prevention and preparedness) and to DPKO (for demining); and responsibility has also been subsequently reassigned for Iraq programmes and the oversight of certain training programmes. These were distractions to the old DHA and certainly not crucial for the execution of its mandate.

Other coordination issues, however, are more central and will undoubtedly be as challenging for the OCHA as they had been for DHA. The creation of a select Steering Committee for the IASC appears potentially useful in order to streamline discussions and make the deliberations of the IASC's inner circle more businesslike and productive. The requirement to avoid an 'open-ended' IASC should be obvious, but it is antithetical to the dominant United Nations culture – the fiction that all agencies, just as all states, are entitled to their say. To permit key organizations to participate more actively than others in decision-making would require overturning the standard operating procedures not only of humanitarian action but of multilateralism more generally.

The 'improvement of the Consolidated Appeal Process' remains vague and requires concrete measures as yet to be agreed in order to get beyond the non-prioritized shopping lists of the past. This arena is one where major pay-offs could take place. One recent assessment of the process in the Great Lakes noted that the CAP 'should be a logical vehicle for strategic coordination, but is far from being so'.[50] What is necessary, and never more so than when cash is in short supply (and emergency funds are now less than half of their peak in 1994–95), is not a stapled-together compendium of agency claims to turf and projects, but rather a hard-headed screening to establish priorities and adjudicate competing claims on scarce resources. The largest UN emergency units with the best fundraising staff and project momentum – especially UNHCR and WFP – fare well under the CAP, whereas those that need it most are those that are the least serviced by it. The process is no guarantee of the appropriate allocation of resources – one of the more glaring lacuna is the paucity of funds for protection, for instance, while hundreds of millions of dollars for emergency assistance are more readily available. Moreover, the CAP is generally biased in favour of UN agencies with requests from NGOs coming later.

Virtually everyone associated with the IASC concedes that the CAP should become far more rigorous, but once again there is no authority to remove the inter-agency chaff from the wheat of essential humanitarian programming. The agencies themselves have incentives to put forward wish-lists and are unlikely to exercise judgement regarding priorities. Hence, OCHA requires independent staff and technicians, along with institutional courage, in order to establish proper sequencing and priorities rather than seconded personnel from other agencies whose job descriptions include protection of their sending agency's turf. Instead of routinely putting forward requests, the OCHA secretariat should prioritize submissions or abandon the process of organizing consolidated appeals.

Perhaps the most doable task concerns the call to improve information efforts that can be an important input for the overall international humanitarian system, in headquarters and in the field. Based on the experience in Rwanda as well as related Internet activities, the OCHA could take the lead in information efforts while encountering little in the way of agency opposition. In particular, the gradual expansion of the IRIN to make daily information bulletins available on other regions in conflict would be a substantial contribution, especially for smaller agencies without the capacity or resources to process such information.

Within the context of the Administrative Committee on Coordination and its subsidiary Consultative Committee on Programme and Operational Questions, the OCHA could play a role in orchestrating humanitarian concerns as the secretariat moves towards experimenting with elements of strategic frameworks for countries in post-war peacebuilding. In 1996 and 1997 an experiment began in Afghanistan, which benefited from the inputs and perspectives of both the UN system and the Bretton Woods institutions. Instead of being led by DPA, DHA was and now the OCHA would appear a more logical choice as focal point for what was called the 'Strategic Framework Mission to Afghanistan'.[51] This is a potentially fruitful context where internal lobbying for humanitarian perspectives should rely upon OCHA's overview of the system as a whole, and strategic and operational coordination are linked. Nonetheless, without any operational activities or interests, the OCHA could play the role of an honest broker in hammering out macro-frameworks. For the moment, however, the point is moot as the process has broken down because of inter-agency bickering.

The main summary recommendation is the most unsatisfactory. It is hardly a foregone conclusion that re-labelling DHA as the 'Office of the ERC' (para. 188) will have an operational impact other than on the letterhead. Ironically, this language was actually used over a half decade earlier in General Assembly resolution 46/182, but the phraseology never caught on during the 1992–97 existence of DHA. The 'back-to-the-future' character of this labelling was perplexing in light of the additional proposal in the report that the General Assembly continue the name game with yet another cosmetic change to 'UN Humanitarian Assistance Coordinator (UNHAC)' (para. 189). After General Assembly resolution 52/72 approved this name change in December, which would have given his office the awkward acronym of OUNHAC, the new Under-Secretary-General for Humanitarian Affairs pleaded to have the simpler OCHA, to which Kofi Annan agreed at the end of January 1998.

The Secretary-General's suggestions ultimately fail to address the essence of organizational orchestration in the field, stating obliquely that 'a lead agency may be designated by the ERC to coordinate complex emergencies'. In short, the report and subsequent intergovernmental decision-making have failed to tackle the most crucial issue – how to get the humanitarian job done at the coal face in complex emergencies, particularly when insecurity reigns and peace operations are in place. The aid establishment in general and emergency relief in particular have been the object of seething criticism;[52] and the latter has been criticized as part of a new political economy of war.[53] The acronyms change – DHA, OERC, OUNHAC, and OCHA – but the unacceptable political and bureaucratic reality remains. To return to the earlier distinctions, rather than moving in the spectrum from coordination by consensus in the direction of coordination by command, the Secretary-General's proposals and General Assembly decisions move from coordination by consensus towards coordination by default. Laissez-faire humanitarianism continues. Only when it suits agencies in a particular operational theatre will better orchestration and synergy result rather than wasteful competition and counterproductivity.

The controversial redesign of the 'new' [sic] OERC was undertaken by a Working Group of the Executive Committee on Humanitarian Affairs.[54] But the problem is more profound than reducing the numbers of DHA professional posts, which has been substantial (about half of the former posts have been reassigned or cut). This result is one that coincides with Jesse Helms's notion of a shrunken UN secretariat, but it hardly makes sense when humanitarian action has become the growth industry fueling UN, NGO and military programming.

One crucial issue for the OCHA is the number of regular budget positions versus those provided by voluntary funds and by secondment from other agencies and Western governments. Clearly, there are trade-offs between involving major agencies and important donors in the day-to-day work of the OCHA versus weakening the independence of the United Nations secretariat. The trend away from regular assessments (only about one-third of the OCHA's positions) towards tied financing for particular nationals or personnel borrowed from particular UN agencies is a mixed blessing. It can provide knowledgeable and additional helping hands but also can undermine the central authority of UN coordination because of so many staff with divided loyalties.

Another crucial administrative issue is where to base the bulk of OCHA staff. New York is the scene for both policy development and advocacy efforts while Geneva is central for operational issues. If the latter are truly secondary, then a liaison office in Geneva should suffice with the bulk of OCHA staff in New York.

In order to get more from the UN system, war victims require an operational capacity and not a humanitarian shell game played by intergovernmental wordsmiths and yet another working honeymoon for the conductor of the UN humanitarian orchestra. After three unsuccessful tries at appropriate staffing, Sergio Vieira de Mello moved from his position as Assistant High Commissioner for Refugees to become the Emergency Relief Coordinator and Under-Secretary-General for Humanitarian Affairs in January 1998. Unlike his predecessors, this career international civil servant from Brazil combines hands-on field cum headquarters experience with humanitarian action as well as political and bureaucratic savvy.

Nonetheless, to be sanguine that value-added can emanate from the OCHA requires overcoming considerable scepticism about the importance of existing institutional structures and ignoring the weight of organizational inertia and of DHA's history. In the hard-hitting prose of three analysts: 'The potential of DHA has long been compromised by a crippling cycle of under-funding and under-performance in addition to a lack of commitment on the part of UN agencies to work out co-ordination arrangements... DHA thus far has not solved the problems that led to its creation in the first place.'[55] The benefit of the doubt should be given to de Mello. Whether donors are willing to provide a fourth honeymoon in six years to the new Under-Secretary-General remains an open question. However, 'coordination light' will be insufficient when the next world-class crisis appears.

Conclusion

The challenges faced by the OCHA are very much the same as those of its predecessor, although the lapse of almost six years could in and of itself make the task of meeting those challenges more difficult. The assumption of DHA's functions by UNHCR would have left everyone grumbling – other UN agencies, NGOs, even some UNHCR staff. Michael Pugh and S. Alex Cunliffe point out that the notion of lead agency itself 'represents a realist "default" position to fill a vacuum in coordination, emerging as an answer to the problem of coordinating the UN's humanitarian missions in the absence of a strong political mechanism'.[56] However, it would also have represented a clear structural shift after years of DHA fumbling. In merely trading a larger DHA for a smaller OCHA, momentum for reform is again dissipated, an essentially weak bureaucratic structure is maintained and meaningful operational coordination in war zones remains elusive.

'Coordination' is a fixation of governments and parliaments – they use its absence to lambaste organizations that try to assist war victims. Within the international public policy lexicon, no expression is more used or misunderstood. Everyone is for it, although no one wishes to be coordinated if it implies any loss of autonomy. But it is just such a compromise that would improve international responses to assist and protect war victims. The recent shell game reveals the low priority of adopting appropriate institutional mechanisms to improve UN humanitarian action – both member states and organizations speak out of two sides of their mouths to reflect politics in the UN goldfish bowl and operational realities.

Is it possible to improve dramatically and build upon the informal combination of factors that have driven the largely perfunctory UN coordination efforts under DHA's and now OCHA's auspices? What are the chances that this office can become the type of permanent rule-breaker that the UN system requires in order to play a meaningful coordination role? The arrival of Sergio Vieira de Mello is encouraging, but is a new personality with support from the Secretary-General enough to transform the centrifugal forces of the United Nations to lead the charge in complex emergencies?

If the answers to these questions are 'no' – and those familiar with UN restructuring would certainly give very long odds against articulating any resounding affirmative responses – governments will ultimately decide whether humanitarian action will be managed by simply ignoring and getting around the new OCHA structure. There are already serious formal and informal coordination efforts among various Western military planners. A handful of mostly Western donor governments puts up virtually all the financial resources for international emergency responses. Should Western capitals, because their governmental representatives at the UN itself are not up to the job, not lead the way? If it is impractical to move towards meaningful centralization – that is, the feudal non-system cannot be made to function as if it were a centrally-organized system – is it not time to look outside the United Nations? NATO would be able and undoubtedly willing to lead coordination efforts in combination with UNHCR and NGOs willing to sign a pact of cooperation for the emergency end of operations, perhaps with the ICRC's close but unofficial cooperation. And donors also could draw more intensively on the World Bank for the other end now that it is reviving the 'reconstruction' part of its original mandate as the International Bank for Reconstruction and Development.[57]

What is potentially most distressing about the existence of a truncated OCHA after the so-called reform of 1997 is what it portends for UN adaptation to the formidable challenges of the post-Cold War world more generally. Humanitarian action is in many ways the soft underbelly of the United Nations. Here, if anywhere, there is support for structural change. If the traumas of northern Iraq, Somalia, Bosnia, Rwanda and Haiti as well as the administrative labours of 1997, gave birth to the OCHA mouse, it is difficult to be sanguine about the ability of the United Nations to be more than a quaint anachronism at the dawn of the twenty-first century.

NOTES

1. For discussions, see Michael Pugh, 'Humanitarianism and Peacekeeping', *Global Society*, Vol.10, No.3, 1996, pp.205–24; Alan James, 'Humanitarian Aid Operations and Peacekeeping', in Eric A. Belgrad and Nitza Nachmias (eds), *The Politics of International Humanitarian Aid Operations*, Westport, Connecticut: Praeger, 1997, pp.53–65; and F.T. Liu, 'Peacekeeping and Humanitarian Assistance', in Leon Gordenker and Thomas G. Weiss (eds), *Soldiers, Peacekeepers and Disasters*, London: Macmillan, 1991, pp.33–51.
2. See Anthony McDermott (ed.), *Humanitarian Force*, Oslo: International Peace Research Institute, 1997, PRIO Report 4/97; and Thomas G. Weiss, 'A Research Note about Military–Civilian Humanitarianism: More Questions than Answers', *Disasters*, Vol.21, No.2, 1997, pp.95–117.
3. For discussions, see Thomas G. Weiss (ed.), *Beyond UN Subcontracting: Task-sharing with Regional Security Arrangements and Service-Providing NGOs*, London: Macmillan, 1998; and Thomas G. Weiss and Leon Gordenker (eds), *NGOs, the UN, and Global Governance*, Boulder: Lynne Rienner, 1996. See also Ettore Grego, *Delegating Peace Operations: Improvisation and Innovation in Georgia and Albania*, New York: UNA–USA, March 1998, International Dialogue on the Enforcement of Security Council Decisions, paper No.7.
4. The acronyms change with confusing rapidity, but this essay uses those in place when events occurred. In 1991, the original resolution 46/182 called for an Emergency Relief Coordinator (ERC), but the first unit was labelled the Department of Humanitarian Affairs (DHA), which existed April 1992–December 1997. The reform proposals and discussions between July 1997 and the General Assembly's decision in December 1997 referred to the revived Office of the Emergency Relief Coordinator (OERC). Following the recommendation of the Secretary-General, General Assembly resolution 52/72 'designated the Emergency Relief Coordinator as the United Nations Humanitarian Assistance Coordinator'. This decision produced the rather infelicitous acronym of OUNHAC for his office. In January 1998 and at the request of the new Under-Secretary-General, the Office for the Coordination of Humanitarian Affairs (OCHA) was approved by the Secretary-General. The head of this office now uses two titles: Under-Secretary-General for Humanitarian Affairs and Emergency Relief Coordinator.
5. Kofi Annan, *Renewing the United Nations: A Programme for Reform*, New York: United Nations, 1997. References are made to paragraph numbers throughout.
6. Larry Minear, U.B.P. Chelliah, Jeff Crisp, John Mackinlay and Thomas G. Weiss, *United Nations Coordination of the International Humanitarian Response to the Gulf Crisis, 1990–1992*, Providence: Watson Institute, 1992, Occasional Paper No.13, p.3.
7. For a discussion, see Thomas G. Weiss, *Military–Civilian Interactions: Intervening in Humanitarian Crises*, Lanham, MD: Rowman & Littlefield, 1999; and Thomas J. Marshall, Philip Kaiser and John Kessweire (eds), *Problems and Solutions in Future Coalition Operations*, Carlisle, PA: US Army War College.
8. This story is told in depth in Thomas G. Weiss, 'Humanitarian Shell Games: Whither UN Reform?', *Security Dialogue*, Vol.29, No.1, March 1998, pp.9–23. Parts of the argument appear here with permission.
9. See Thomas G. Weiss and Amir Pasic, 'Reinventing UNHCR: Enterprising Humanitarians in the Former Yugoslavia', *Global Governance*, Vol.3, No.1, 1997, pp.41–57.
10. Thomas G. Weiss, 'Overcoming the Somalia: "Operation Rekindle Hope?"' *Global Governance*, Vol.1, No.2, 1995, pp.171–87; and 'Military–Civilian Humanitarianism: "The Age of Innocence" Is Over', *International Peacekeeping*, Vol.2, No.2, 1995, pp.157–74.
11. James Ingram, 'The Future Architecture for International Humanitarian Assistance', in Thomas G. Weiss and Larry Minear (eds), *Humanitarianism Across Borders: Sustaining Civilians in Times of War*, Boulder: Lynne Rienner, 1993, pp.174–93. This option seems

infeasible for a number of reasons. First, there is the implausibility of altering the ICRC's Swiss character. Second, there is the ICRC's unwillingness to budge from its principle of consent, which by definition will be a handicap in enforcement operations. Finally, its ferocious need to maintain autonomy is hardly conducive to being the servant of governments. The interested reader is referred to 'The ICRC's "Avenir Project": Challenges, Mission and Strategy', document dated 12 December 1997.

12. US Permanent Mission to the United Nations, 'Readying the United Nations for the Twenty-First Century: Some "UN-21" Proposals for Consideration', undated 'non-paper' of July 1995. This theme also appeared in the 'Address by Secretary of State Warren Christopher to the 50th Session of the United Nations General Assembly', 25 September 1995.

13. Jan Pronk, 'Statement in the General Debate in the Second Committee', New York, 14 October 1996, Permanent Mission of the Kingdom of the Netherlands to the United Nations, p.7.

14. See Joint Evaluation of Emergency Assistance to Rwanda, *The International Response to Conflict and Genocide: Lessons from the Rwanda Experience*, Copenhagen: Joint Evaluation of Emergency Assistance to Rwanda, March 1996, Volume 3; 'Humanitarian Aid and Effects', pp.159–61; and 'Synthesis Report', p.58.

15. See, for example, Erskine Childers with Brian Urquhart, *Renewing the United Nations System*, Uppsala: Dag Hammarskjöld Foundation, 1994; and Gareth Evans, *Cooperating for Peace*, London: Allen and Unwin, 1993. For criticisms of the disorganized humanitarian system by the late Frederick C. Cuny, see 'Humanitarian Assistance in the Post-Cold War Era', in Weiss and Minear (eds), *Humanitarianism Across Borders*, pp.151–69.

16. *The State of the World's Refugees 1993: The Challenge of Protection*, New York: Penguin Books, 1993; and Gil Loescher, *Beyond Charity: International Cooperation and the Global Refugee Crisis*, New York: Oxford University Press, 1993. This lament continues as a theme in *The State of the World's Refugees 1995: In Search of Solutions,* New York: Oxford University Press, 1995 and *The State of the World's Refugees 1997–98: A Humanitarian Agenda*, New York: Oxford University Press, 1997.

17. William Shawcross, 'UNHCR: Criticisms and Challenges', draft dated 4 July 1997.

18. Myron Wiener, 'The Clash of Norms: Dilemmas in Refugee Policies', in *Journal of Refugee Studies, Vol.11*, No.4, 1998, pp.1–21.

19. Larry Minear and Thomas G. Weiss, 'Groping and Coping in the Gulf Crisis: Discerning the Shape of a New Humanitarian Order', *World Policy Journal*, Vol.9, No.4, Fall/Winter 1992, pp.755–76.

20. In fact, UNDRO in the mid-1980s and until its demise devoted a major proportion of its human resources to civil strife.

21. Raimo Väyrynen, *The Age of Humanitarian Emergencies*, Helsinki: World Institute for Development Economics Research, June 1996, Research for Action 25.

22. Cindy Collins and Thomas G. Weiss, *An Overview and Assessment of 1989–1996 Peace Operations Publications*, Providence: Watson Institute, 1997, Occasional Paper No.28.

23. Frederick C. Cuny, 'Dilemmas of Military Involvement in Humanitarian Relief', in Leon Gordenker and Thomas G. Weiss (eds), *Soldiers, Peacekeepers and Disasters*, London: Macmillan, 1991, pp.52–81.

24. John B. Hunt, 'OOTW: A Concept in Flux', *Military Review,* Vol.76, No.5, September–October 1996, pp.3–9.

25. Jarat Chopra, 'Back to the Drawing Board', *Bulletin of the Atomic Scientists,* Vol.51, No.2, March/April 1995, pp.29–35 and 'The Space of Peace Maintenance', *Political Geography,* Vol.15, No.3/4, March/April 1996, pp.335–57. See also his *Peace Maintenance: The Evolution of International Political Authority*, London: Routledge, forthcoming.

26. Chris Seiple, *The U.S. Military/NGO Relationship in Humanitarian Interventions*, Carlisle, PA: US Army War College, 1996, pp.v–vi. See also Robert D. Kaplan, 'Fort Leavenworth and the Eclipse of Nationhood', *The Atlantic Monthly*, September 1996, pp.75–90.

27. See Jon Bennet, *Meeting Needs: NGO Coordination in Practice*, London: Earthscan, 1995 and *NGO Coordination at Field Level: A Handbook*, Oxford: Parchment, 1994; Larry Minear and Thomas G. Weiss, *Mercy Under Fire: War and the Global Humanitarian Community*, Boulder: Westview, 1995; Thomas G. Weiss and Cindy Collins, *Humanitarian Challenges*

and Intervention: The Dilemmas of Help, Boulder: Westview, 1996; Jonathan Moore, *The UN and Complex Emergencies,* Geneva: UNRISD, 1996; and Edward Marks, *Complex Emergencies: Bureaucratic Arrangements in the U.N. Secretariat,* Washington, DC: National Defense University, 1996.

28. Adam Roberts, *Humanitarian Action in War: Aid, Protection and Impartiality in a Policy Vacuum,* Oxford: Oxford University Press, 1996, Adelphi Paper 305.

29. See the essays in Olara Otunnu and Michael W. Doyle (eds), *Peacemaking and Peacekeeping for the New Century,* Lanham, Maryland: Rowman & Littlefield, 1998.

30. See *The State of the World's Refugees, 1997–1998.*

31. UNDRO was headed by an Under-Secretary-General. However, Boutros-Ghali had cut dramatically the number of under-secretaries-general as one of his first administrative decisions. Thus, it was not a foregone conclusion that the Emergency Relief Coordinator would occupy the same rank as the Disaster Relief Coordinator.

32. Much of the controversy surrounded the fear by developing countries of a humanitarian 'Trojan Horse' that would eventually be used to override their sovereignty. For a discussion, see Mario Bettati, *Le Droit d'Ingérence: Mutation de l'Ordre International,* Paris: Odile Jacob, 1996.

33. Jacques Cuénod, 'Coordinating United Nations Humanitarian Assistance', *RPG Focus,* Washington, DC: Refugee Policy Group, 1993.

34. Brian Urquhart and Erskine Childers, *A World in Need of Leadership: Tomorrow's United Nations – A Fresh Appraisal,* Uppsala: Hammarskjöld Foundation, 1996.

35. Gil Loescher, 'The United Nations High Commissioner for Refugees in the Post-Cold War Era', in Belgrad and Nachmias (eds), *The Politics of International Humanitarian Aid Operations,* pp.157–70, 164.

36. Andrew S. Natsios, *U.S. Foreign Policy and the Four Horsemen of the Apocalypse: Humanitarian Relief in Complex Emergencies,* Westport, CT: Praeger, 1997, p.83.

37. Thomas G. Weiss, David P. Forsythe and Roger A. Coate, *The United Nations and Changing World Politics,* Boulder: Westview, 1997, second edition.

38. For a promotional view of its own activities, see UN Department of Humanitarian Affairs, *Humanitarian Report 1997,* New York: United Nations, 1997.

39. Joint Evaluation of Emergency Assistance to Rwanda, *The International Response to Conflict and Genocide: Lessons from the Rwandan Experience,* Copenhagen: Joint Evaluation of Emergency Assistance to Rwanda, March 1995, 5 volumes; and Larry Minear and Philippe Guillot, *Soldiers to the Rescue: Humanitarian Lessons from Rwanda,* Paris: Organization for Economic Cooperation and Development, 1996.

40. US Mission to the United Nations, *Global Humanitarian Emergencies, 1997,* documented dated April 1997, pp.15.

41. See Shepard Forman, 'Underwriting Humanitarian Assistance: Mobilizing Resources for an Effective Response', in Kevin Cohill (ed.), *A Framework for Survival: Health, Human Rights, and Humanitarian Assistance in Conflict and Disasters,* New York: Basic Books, forthcoming.

42. One of the main drawbacks of the CERF is the need to repay funds, which UN agencies have trouble persuading donors to undertake post facto. Indeed, in 1996 only $2 million was disbursed.

43. Monographs published by the Humanitarianism and War Project at Brown University's Watson Institute document, among other things, the host of coordination problems, especially those related to the dynamics of humanitarian action at the interface with military operations under UN auspices. Case studies published to date include Chechnya, Nagorno-Karabakh, Haiti, Georgia, Liberia, the former Yugoslavia, Cambodia, Central America, the Gulf Crisis and Sudan. These are available at the following electronic address: http://www.brown.edu/Departments/Watson_Institute/H_W.

44. Antonio Donini, *The Policies of Mercy: UN Coordination in Afghanistan, Mozambique and Rwanda,* Providence: Watson Institute, 1996, Occasional Paper No.22, pp.14. This document builds on an earlier typology in Antonio Donini and Norah Niland, *Lessons Learned: A Report on the Coordination of Humanitarian Activities in Rwanda,* New York: DHA, November 1994.

45. Sue Lantze, Bruce Jones and Mark Duffield, *Strategic Humanitarian Co-ordination in the Great Lakes Region, 1996–1997: An Independent Assessment for the Inter-Agency Standing Committee*, New York: IASC draft, March 1998, p.62.
46. Press release SG/2037, ORG/1239 of 16 July 1997. Analysts other than the UN's public relations staff have also been laudatory. See, for example, Jeffrey Laurenti, 'A Critical Assessment of the Secretary-General's Reform Program', UN Association of the USA, document dated 12 August 1997.
47. *Report of the Secretary-General on the Work of the Organization (1997)*, doc. A/52/1, para. 106.
48. Quoted by Lautze, Jones and Duffield, *Strategic Humanitarian Co-ordination*, p.7.
49. See Larry Minear, David Cortright, Julia Wagler, George A. Lopez and Thomas G. Weiss, *Toward More Humane and Effective Sanctions Management*, New York: DHA, 1997.
50. Lautze, Jones and Duffield, *Strategic Humanitarian Co-ordination*, p.59.
51. Inter-Agency Mission to Islamabad and Afghanistan, *Draft Strategic Framework for International Assistance in Afghanistan*, New York: IASC, draft dated 15 October 1997.
52. See, for example, Michael Maren, *The Road to Hell: The Ravaging Effects of Foreign Aid and International Charity*, New York: Free Press, 1997; Alex de Waal and Rakiya Omaar, *Humanitarianism Unbound*, London, African Rights, 1994, Discussion Paper No.5; David Sogge (ed.), *Compassion and Calculation: The Business of Private Foreign Aid*, London: Pluto Press, 1996; and Peter J. Burnell, *Charity, Politics and the Third World*, New York: Harvester Wheatleaf, 1991. For a discussion of the recent literature and evolving principles and thoughts, see Chr. Michelsen Institute, *Humanitarian Assistance and Conflict*, Bergen: Chr. Michelsen Institute, 1997.
53. See Mark Duffield, 'The Political Economy of Internal War: Asset Transfer and the Internationalisation of Public Welfare in the Horn of Africa', in Joanna Macrae and Anthony Zwi (eds), *War and Hunger: Rethinking International Responses to Complex Emergencies*, London: Zed Books, 1994, pp.50–69; and Mark Duffield, 'NGO Relief in War Zones: Towards an Analysis of the New Aid Paradigm', *Third World Quarterly*, Vol.18, No.3, 1997, pp.527–542. See also: Alex de Waal, *Famine Crimes: Politics & the Disaster Relief Industry in Africa*, Oxford: James Currey, 1997; François Jean and Christophe Rufin (eds), *Economies des Guerres Civiles*, Paris: Hachette, 1996; and François Jean, 'Le Triomphe Ambigu de l'Aide Humanitaire', *Revue Tiers Monde*, Vol.38, No.151, July–September 1997, pp.641–58.
54. Nigel Fisher chair), 'Recommendations on the Functions and Structure of the New Office of the UN Emergency Relief Coordinator', unpublished document dated 7 September 1997.
55. Lautze, Jones and Duffield, *Strategic Humanitarian Co-ordination*, pp.55–6.
56. Michael Pugh and S. Alex Cunliffe, 'The Lead Agency Concept in Humanitarian Assistance', *Security Dialogue*, Vol.28, No.1, March 1997, p.17.
57. See *A Framework for World Bank Involvement in Post-Conflict Reconstruction*, Washington, DC: World Bank, 1997.

Complex Emergencies, Peacekeeping and the World Food Programme

RAYMOND F. HOPKINS

The World Food Programme's largest mission has evolved in the last decade from development to disaster relief. In particular, the rise of emergency food aid delivered in response to civil disorders has presented new challenges. This has led to substantial organizational challenges. Coordination with UN and NGO humanitarian agencies has grown, logistical capacity has adapted to difficult requirements, and strategies for working in an insecure environment have been developed. The reliance on emergency relief makes WFP operations and funding more dependent on unpredictable political events. Owing to this evolution and the variability of emergency needs, WFP's future direction and role in the UN system remain important issues.

The demand for UN intervention to provide emergency feeding to refugees and displaced persons fleeing domestic wars in the 1990s has substantially altered the World Food Programme. WFP's modal mission has evolved from development to disaster relief. In 1977, 19 per cent of its food aid commitments were for emergencies. Over three-quarters of this food was targeted to respond to physical calamities such as droughts. Twenty years later, in 1997, 85 per cent of WFP commitments went to emergency operations. Furthermore, three-quarters of these resources were committed in response to 'man-made' disasters.[1]

WFP was perhaps the most affected of UN agencies as a result of the growth of emergency responses. Growth in emergency operations also changed WFP far more than it changed the organizations of bilateral food aid providers such as the US government or the European Union, or NGOs such as World Vision or CARE. Thus, while world-wide food aid donations shifted towards humanitarian response, this shift was far less pronounced among bilateral donors. Global food aid flows for emergency relief moved from 15 per cent in the 1970s to 30 per cent in the mid-1990s, doubling the share; for WFP the resource shift was nearer four-fold.

This essay reviews the dramatic shift in WFP orientation towards emergency feeding, particularly in 'complex emergencies' in which political, military and humanitarian missions are undertaken. It considers

Raymond Hopkins is Richter Professor of Political Science at Swarthmore College, Pennsylvania.

the effects of this shift on the WFP as an organization and on the efficient use of food aid for recipients. The transformation of WFP from a development organization towards a humanitarian response agency, while still on-going, has already had substantial consequences for its operations. It has entailed a greater attention to shorter-term, more costly interventions. There has been an attendant reduction in capacity-building collaborations with developing countries. More poor countries that are relatively stable are getting fewer resources. Uses of food aid for targeted, sustainable hunger reduction projects have been curtailed. In this regard, while WFP operates in ways that are similar to other parts of the UN system, the special nature of food aid as a less fungible resource than cash, and one more conventionally linked to immediate relief, makes the changes in WFP more pronounced.

Two external factors in particular have driven WFP away from its original mandate. First, WFP's mission has been heavily affected by shrinking global aid contributions. Since 1992 cash and food for regular WFP programmes stopped growing. As a consequence, it was necessary to de-earmark funds for development projects already committed, and projects in the pipeline were set aside. The cash reserves of the programme became nearly exhausted. Coinciding with this tightening of regular resources, a second factor – the growing demands that WFP launch humanitarian responses for people devastated by a rise in anarchical strife – was accompanied by increased resources provided for this purpose. Thus WFP was drawn towards an enhanced role as a crisis response agency. By bringing food to rescue people fleeing conflict, the agency not only serves the human rights objective of the right not to starve, but also plays a supportive part in UN peacekeeping.

Background

Since its establishment in 1963, the World Food Programme has been the United Nations' principal arm to provide food aid. Three broad stages of development have occurred in the agency's work. The first, 1963–75, was marked by growth and consolidation around the use of food aid for development projects. The second, culminating in the 1980s, entailed increased autonomy of WFP and sharpened dedication to development objectives. Since the late 1980s a third stage has occurred. WFP has moved deeper into providing food in emergencies, principally ones where civil conflict creates refugees and exacerbates famine.

The founding vision of WFP was shaped by American and Canadian internationalists. Food surpluses, used in the 1950s as bilateral food aid, were seen as a valuable additional resource for UN work. Moreover, it was believed, multilateral management of food aid could avoid political and economic priorities that prevailed in bilateral allocations. Indeed, the UN context could encourage the design of 'model projects' in which food aid would be used to have a maximum impact on long-term well-being.[2]

Begun as a small, experimental effort under the joint oversight of the UN in New York and the FAO in Rome, WFP during the 1960s and 1970s made steady advances in size and diversity with regular growth in pledged resources. While some food aid for emergencies was provided, these tended to be *ad hoc* instances, often linked to shortages experienced in countries with existing longer-term development projects. The World Food Conference of 1974 marked a critical juncture in WFP's history. Its governance and mandate were overhauled. Its inter-governmental steering committee was replaced by a broader-gauged parliament – the Committee on Food Aid, Policies and Programmes. The CFA's mandate included global policy leadership for the use of all food aid. During the early 1970s when surpluses first disappeared, surplus food disposal – once a major fear because of its potential for trade distortions – became a peripheral concern for multilateral diplomacy. Donor funding became less linked to agricultural ministry budgeting recommendations and oversight. Food aid for sustainable development became the central objective for most governments.

This situation launched the second era in WFP's history. After 1975 the organization's voluntary contributions continued to grow; and by the 1980s WFP had become the largest UN agency in resource transfers; its assistance was second only to that of the World Bank among multilateral bodies. Its portfolio of projects likewise expanded. These ranged widely in size and purpose. Thus its pledged food and cash resources supported projects that aided general development, such as road building and repair, as well as specific efforts to alleviate hunger, such as targeted feeding in health clinics.

With WFP's growth by the 1980s, stakeholders from rich and poor countries alike expected expanded impacts from its work. The WFP was called upon, through delegates' statements at CFA meetings, to increase its development functions. In particular, many donors offered support for projects that used food to create long-term assets – roads, irrigation ditches, grain storage capabilities. It was also asked to expand efforts to fight hunger through newer types of development projects and/or quicker responses to rescuing countries faced with emergencies. One group of donors, largely small ones led by the Nordic group, were sceptical of development uses of food aid. They preferred that emergency relief be the central aim for food aid, saving people from famine and destitution. At the same time, both external and internal critics wanted WFP to do its work more effectively, recasting its operations in the light of criticism that arose in the 1960s and

1970s that food aid created disincentives and constituted a 'moral hazard' for policy making.[3] To meet these demands WFP sought and won greater autonomy from the FAO. A series of legal and political battles within the UN system in the 1980s gave WFP by 1991 independence in staff management, accounting and mission priority. By the end of this second historical period, under James Ingram as Executive Director, WFP not only increased its autonomy but also sharpened its development portfolio through increased project and policy analysis. Food recipients were distinguished from project beneficiaries; local purchase of food was emphasized where possible. The latter was a measure justified more to assist income and food system stability in a recipient country or region than to reduce transaction costs. In addition, throughout the period, WFP enhanced its logistical capacity to deliver food, taking on the broad management of moving food from donors to inland points of end use in recipient countries. 'Monetization' (selling food in the recipient's local market) became a common practice, at least to cover local costs of inland transport, storage and handling. The central theme of this second WFP stage was to target food aid to food-insecure populations in ways that achieved a sustainable reduction of hunger. Emergency food aid, more controlled by the FAO, was consciously limited, at least until the food crises in sub-Saharan Africa in the mid-1980s.

In emergencies, delivery of food has substantial additional costs. The overhead costs and increased logistic outlays were not easily covered. To meet its regular administration and transport costs the WFP had set a goal for donor pledges that one-third should be in cash. The biggest donor, the US, never followed this guide. Cash from food importing states, such as Saudi Arabia, was a major help in the 1980s. Such cash flows diminished by the end of the 1980s. Sometimes they were replaced by food donations such as dates from Saudi Arabia (used in the Afghan emergency.) In this era cash resources were also limited by a structural conflict between the major source of funding, industrialized countries, and recipient countries. The level of cash support from rich states was a major element in CFA debates since the 1970s. Poorer countries – often grouped as the 'G-77' states – regularly sought more resources. They felt they deserved a fairer share of the world's resources. Though food aid *per se* was not a high priority in their quest, food shortages and chronic hunger were growing world concerns and thus gaining attention.[4] An organizational goal in this second stage, then, became the mobilization of cash resources to enable flexible and efficient projects – both in emergency and long-term development contexts.

The third stage of WFP's evolution was foreshadowed by the Ethiopian emergency feeding operations in 1984–86. In the 1980s humanitarian disasters, while growing, were seen as a distraction from WFP's main task.

WFP development staff, already directing development operations in countries suffering emergency needs, were frequently able to add to their work the oversight of emergency operations. To do this the existing administrative capacities were diverted, stocks in place quickly released, additional food for the emergency mobilized, and local management capacity was augmented by more staff and transport vehicles. With some lag, additional imported volumes of food arrived to serve both the emergency feeding operation and to replenish stocks earmarked for development projects.

This pattern has changed. Since the end of the Cold War, internal conflicts have drawn the UN into more difficult and expensive peace-seeking efforts than it had previously undertaken in its entire history. The budget for peacekeeping grew six-fold between the 1989–91 era and the 1993–95 period. Into the peacekeeping missions, along with military personnel, went social programmes targeted for emergency relief. Perforce WFP operations grew alongside these peacekeeping missions.

This growth in peacekeeping and humanitarian spending occurred even as budget constraints were tightening. Central foreign affairs spending in the US and other OECD states was about to decline. The end of the Cold War, together with the rise to power of neo-liberal political coalitions in donor countries that opposed welfare functions of the state, undercut support for foreign assistance, including food aid. At one time food aid played a visible role in East–West political competition, and political factors shaped its allocation. The loss of this diplomatic rationale for aid occurred incrementally during the 1970s. For example, as Cuba and Vietnam became WFP recipients, interests in donor states of the foreign policy community visibly shrank. Attacks on welfare state policies in the domestic politics of donors also grew in the 1980s. This ideological shift was a second change. Less support also resulted from a third factor, the demise of strong farm lobbies and agricultural policy reform. This change became most apparent in the 1990s, when incentives to produce food surpluses, which had been part of US and European domestic farm programmes, were reduced. Preventing surpluses from eroding prices had given farmers a strong reason to support food aid. The government burden of holding surpluses added an incentive, making the budget costs of food aid less than that for cash aid for the largest donors. These three changes, working together, reduced international and domestic pressure to provide food aid. In time, the resulting decline in food aid was reflected in both domestic budget allocations and international commitments by the mid-1990s.

The past roles of such economic and political elements shaping WFP resources are visible, for example, in the history of the Food Aid Convention. The FAC originated in 1967 as a mechanism to share the

burden of food aid among OECD countries; it was extended in 1980 with a
minimum commitment raised from 4.5 to 7.6 million tons. Over half was
pledged by the US.[5] The FAC created an international legal presumption
that its signatories guaranteed the provision of a minimum annual tonnage
of food aid, and the WFP was the conduit of choice for many signatories.
As a pivotal provider, the size of the US's FAC pledge made the WFP
vulnerable when the US made a sharp reduction in 1995. The total FAC
pledge fell to 5.4 million tons as the US, Canada and Australia all
downsized their pledges. Much food aid flows outside this convention;
however, the decline in total food aid proved even more precipitous than the
convention's 2 million ton decline. Overall, from 1993 to 1996 global food
aid deliveries shrank from 16 million to 6 million tons. Even though WFP's
share of total world deliveries reached an all-time high of 35 per cent, the
tonnage provided by WFP had to decline.[6] This decline in global and WFP
food aid continued in 1997–98.[7]

The only reliable rationale for food aid that remains is emergency
feeding. The shift towards this role for food aid began at the time of internal
wars in Ethiopia and Afghanistan. It mushroomed when a growing need to
feed refugees and displaced persons arose in other countries with civil
conflicts: Angola, Iraq, Liberia, Mozambique, Rwanda and Somalia. All
became challenges for WFP action. In the first half of the 1990s, as
development resources were tightening, the willingness of donors to
provide emergency resources kept the WFP growing as an agency. In fact,
donor countries and the WFP concurred that changes to make WFP more a
humanitarian agency were in order. A streamlined Executive Board
replaced the CFA as the governing assembly. A new formula for calculating
overhead costs of emergency food aid was developed. Personnel
experienced in emergencies were sent to the field with expanded authority.

As emergency feeding became a WFP priority, donors also reduced their
resources provided for development efforts. The shift to emergencies should
not be interpreted as diverting food aid from development, *per se*. In
practice WFP stocks positioned in a country for use in a development
project have been diverted to emergency use for decades. In the past such
stocks were normally replaced. In fact, this has become more uncertain.
Complex emergencies occur in situations where foreign aid for
development work – road-building, education, research – is invariably
disrupted and most often suspended. Unlike weather-induced, short-term
emergencies, which occur in countries with low capacity to adapt to
production shortfalls, complex emergencies last longer – sometimes years.
Thus development is essentially halted. In Liberia, Sudan and Somalia this
has certainly been true. Emergency food aid could once be seen as a way to
rescue development opportunities, creating better outcomes for future

development projects. This new form of emergency relief, however, is substantially different from natural disaster cases when development projects could often continue and even be used as a vehicle for emergency responses.

The real issue is whether donor resources for WFP development projects have been reduced because donors reallocated their budget outlays or because they decided to simply reduce regular food aid (or even all ODA). Andrew Natsios, for instance, argues that the large US food contributions to emergencies did *not* reduce development-oriented food aid. 'These funds would not have been used for sustainable development,' Natsios argues. He believes regular food aid is not as politically popular as food for emergencies.[8] Thus the decline of all foreign assistance in the 1990s, led by changes in the US, in fact initially had less impact on food aid than on other assistance budget categories. Since 1995, however, food aid budgeted for development, in real terms, has shrunk; within this funding, moreover, amounts earmarked as available for shifts to emergencies has increased.

UN reform mandates also had an institutional effect on WFP in this third era. Coordination of WFP within the UN system in the first two eras had been closest with the FAO; and its projects in school feeding or maternal child health centres were often joint efforts with UNESCO and WHO. System-wide reforms in the UN have long called for improved coordination mechanisms. In the 1980s this led, in particular, to increased WFP responsibility to coordinate its development efforts with UNDP leadership. More recently, certainly after 1991, WFP coordinated its growing humanitarian relief portfolio with DHA (now OCHA), UNHCR, and UNICEF. Further, as a result of the resource changes in 1992–98, as well as the UN strategy to focus on least-developed countries, WFP decreased the number of countries in which it operates, gave greater organizational efforts to operations in complex emergencies, and launched new relationships both in the UN system and with NGOs.

In this new era, emergency food aid can be understood not only as a response to people in desperation but also as a resource for bolstering peacekeeping efforts and for initiating a restoration of development activities. The emergency-humanitarian era reinforced mandates already built into WFP (and also in other food agency mandates) of moving from relief towards development outcomes within emergency operations as soon as practicable. This third historical stage, coming amidst reform and budget reductions in the UN, has resulted in a re-oriented WFP. Its operations and goals have altered, its character and morale have been reconfigured and new, often daunting, field tasks have been assumed.

Complex Emergency Situations

In November 1992 a ship carrying WFP food to Somalia was shelled in Mogadishu harbour by warring clan factions. This unrestrained violence, threatening life-saving food headed towards thousands of desperate refugees, galvanized world opinion. UN and NGO efforts to assist populations facing starvation in Somalia had for months been hampered by the internecine fighting among clan factions. Some UN workers' lives had already been lost. The shelling was a threshold event. Within a week the US and other countries came to support expanded external intervention. This resulted in a UN mandate calling for coercive military intervention. Troops of the United States joined other UN forces. Together these military forces linked coercive authority with UN and bilateral food deliveries. The UN military force, coordinating with WFP and non-government agencies, sought to restore sufficient order to allow for the relief and resettlement of displaced Somalis. Thus humanitarian efforts in a human-created and 'complex' emergency grew to link food deliveries and coercion. As in Iraq earlier, military deployment and refugee feeding operations were combined to serve as mechanisms for restoring peaceful order. Not all collaboration between food relief and military deployment need fall within the purview of Chapter 7 intervention with its peace enforcement goals. Truce observance and other less intrusive peacekeeping missions can also link militarized situations with food relief, as in Angola, Bosnia and Mozambique.

The Somali case is paradigmatic, however. It illustrates the numerous elements in any effort by WFP to use its food resources, including intelligence, procurement, logistics and management. Various other UN bodies can use and share these elements to address emergency needs in situations where peacekeeping is a problem. In Sierra Leone/Liberia, Afghanistan, Mozambique, Eastern Congo (Zaire), Sudan, Bosnia and elsewhere WFP emergency relief supplies have, therefore, been a part of an overall peacekeeping effort. By peacekeeping in this essay I include all situations in which relief efforts occur under conditions of civil violence. Perhaps it should be limited to cases in which external military personnel are present for purposes of advancing public order among the population. This would exclude cases such as Ethiopia (1980s) or Sudan (1980s to the present) in which insurrection was ongoing and interfered with relief efforts. A more inclusive definition, however, is preferable. Thus countries such as Sudan, where UN military intervention has not occurred, pose very similar political and military constraints for WFP. In Sudan, protracted conflict threatens the safety of relief workers, and that country holds the largest number of victims of civil conflict who have experienced famine in recent years. In 1998 over four million people in Southern Sudan are estimated to be displaced and at risk.

The costs of UN peacekeeping grew from $480 million in 1991 to over $3 billion in 1993–95. Since then (by 1997) these costs have declined to less than half that amount. Peacekeeping missions, as noted, are not always present in conflict situations where UN humanitarian agencies are called upon to work. In Sudan, Rwanda or Afghanistan, WFP and other UN agencies working to alleviate suffering operate with difficulty. In these complex insecure areas lacking UN military forces to protect them or to provide logistical assistance, they have required considerable additional operational support. No wonder the budgets of UN agencies, including WFP, UNDP and UNICEF, grew from $4 billion to over $6 billion in 1994–97. This change reflected the rising costs for the principal UN agencies to operate in areas of turmoil. The increase also faces uncertain sustainability. Furthermore, high budget levels related to peacekeeping concerns create hesitation to commit to long-term projects.[9]

WFP Efforts in the Context of Peacekeeping

There is an array of terms used for UN responses to internal war. Peacekeeping, the term for the most common UN role historically, was previously reserved for cases where UN troops were present to assist parties to agreements achieve greater reliability for their accord. As the demand for UN action has grown since 1990, the functions for UN forces have also grown. UN 'peacekeeping' discussions are now supplemented with various other terms, many overlapping in their reference: peace creation, peace enforcement, peace maintenance, peacemaking. As noted above, this essay ignores the distinctions among these terms and the situations to which they refer. It does not matter greatly to WFP's role which of the different UN mandates and rules of engagement have been adopted for the deployment of force or even if external UN or other military have arrived. The deterioration of physical safety in an area is the critical element. It changes the character of operations. Efforts to supply food to a targeted populace has higher costs and more food disappearances when there are physical threats to the lives of UN staff and to the targets of their relief efforts. This change occurs when UN military forces are not present, as in Iraq, Sudan or Afghanistan. It also occurs when forces are present in a country, but operate principally to facilitate a transition from civil strife, as in Angola or Mozambique. It occurs in cases where more classical peacekeeping is attempted, as in the early stages of the Somalian, Rwandan and Bosnian crises. And it occurs in cases where more coercive peacekeeping is applied, as in Iraq or Somalia after 1992 (but not Rwanda, after early peacekeeping failed). While the added costs and losses in such cases vary, all challenge

WFP with a common problem – working in a dangerous environment.[10] Furthermore, all cases involve using food to rescue people rather than to assist in economic development.

In all such cases, peacekeeping should be made easier thanks to the assistance provided to refugees. By overseeing the stabilization and relief needs of an endangered population, UN and NGO agencies reduce the chaos of a military conflict. Non-combatants flood into camps, where their temporary human needs are met. Camps provide basic order and structure to people's lives, making the problem of displaced peoples more manageable as steps are taken towards ending war. In Bosnia, for example, WFP and UNHCR efforts reduced the flood of refugees crossing into Germany, Austria and elsewhere in Europe. Thus among the principal benefits of humanitarian efforts for peacekeeping are enhanced stability in a region and reduced burdens on neighbouring states. Literally millions of lives have been improved, even saved, by WFP humanitarian efforts in over a dozen countries during the 1990s.

Principles that shaped development uses of food aid can be used effectively in these longer-term emergencies. Establishing conditions for resettlement and employment in peaceful areas, undertaken for those who have taken refuge in camps, helps restore stability. Purchasing and using local goods in emergencies also can help local economies, reducing possible tensions between refugees and permanent residents in an area, as well as preventing imported food from being a destabilizing influence on local markets. In Somalia, for example, in 1993 once peaceful conditions were improved, a plan for helping local food markets was implemented. Imported rice was sold in Mogadishu, increasing the food supply for urban dwellers, including militia members who, if hungry, might steal food; and the funds generated were used to purchase maize produced by Somali farmers near refugee camps for feeding the displaced people in these camps their more familiar food. Thus dietary preferences, urban food supply and remunerative farm gate prices were all enhanced by using a development-oriented food aid management principle.

The transition towards sustainable livelihood and a secure environment is not without peril. Especially in the initial rescue stages, the temporary provision of food to victims of a disintegrating domestic order may prolong or exacerbate the conflict and add to the costs of peacekeeping as well. Hutu genocide leaders who took up residence in relief camps in the Eastern Congo, for example, used the food and supplies provided for needy refugees as a cloak to extract a tax on relief efforts. Eventually, from the protection of the camps, they were able to launch military attacks. The inability to separate fighters from victims in such camps invites such extortion from UN resources by those inside camps. Another form of rent-seeking, taxing the external feeding effort, is through offers of protection to otherwise insecure camps. Here, local militia, as in Somalia and the Congo (in the latter case by troops loyal to Mobutu) learn to sell services to UN and NGO agencies. These practices can have destructive effects on peacekeeping. The work of UNHCR, along with WFP and other UN agencies, for example, may have prolonged insecurities in Rwanda and even provided incentives for the coalition under Kabilia that eventually successfully overthrew the Mobutu regime. The employment by the UN of Zairian military personnel around the Goma area had indirect and dramatic effects on UN peacekeeping.

Such cases demonstrate that the humanitarian goal of rescue and the peacekeeping goal of the suppression of violence can come into conflict. Existing UN arrangements offer little hope of overcoming such outcomes that work at cross-purposes. The disjointedness of relief efforts makes this very difficult, at least in recent experience. UN organizational structure has been a formidable barrier to concerted policy in humanitarian responses, especially in complex emergencies. The change of DHA to a coordinating function may help reduce what Natsios described it in 1996 as the

> highly decentralized, feudal nature of the response systems the UN system had: three central headquarters staff directorates in the secretariat (humanitarian affairs, peacekeeping operations and political affairs); the big four UN organizations (UNDP, UNICEF, WFP and UNHCR); 40 major relief NGOs; the ICRC (and the Red Cross Movement, which is an organizationally discrete entity); the military units making up international forces (all of which report back operationally to their military command structures in their home countries rather than to the UN force commander in the field); the US State Department and foreign ministries of other interested countries; and the foreign disaster response offices of donor countries (OFDA and ECHO). If one were present at the creation of this Byzantine system, one could not have created a more complex and convoluted structure.[11]

The Executive Director's personal authority is a vital element in strengthening WFP's capacity to relieve problems of complex agency relations or other barriers caused by competing interests among combatants. These often occur in peace promotion situations rather than peacekeeping where UN troops are already deployed. Thus, Executive Director James Ingram played a key role in opening a port for the use of food aid to Ethiopian refugee camps in the 1980s, and Catherine Bertini, Executive Director since 1992, has led efforts to target and deliver emergency food aid in North Korea. Both humanitarian undertakings involved negotiations with Marxist regimes to rationalize efforts. Both fit larger peacekeeping functions. Reducing desperation from food insecurity serves as a conflict prevention measure. Stabilizing food shortages can be an important phase in a comprehensive peacekeeping undertaking. With sufficient food for those with guns, they have far less incentive to use violence to steal food from others. While relief operations themselves, especially ones involving camps, may complicate peacekeeping, food security itself is a natural ally in emergency efforts to restore peace.

Challenges of Complex Emergencies

With the rise of its involvement in complex emergencies the World Food Programme has faced three challenges. These challenges have been, first, to coordinate the provisioning of food aid relief from multiple sources and agencies; second, to meet extraordinary logistical tasks; and third, to operate within an insecure environment.

Coordination

The number of instances in which coordination occurs between WFP and other humanitarian agencies, including non-government organizations, has grown. In complex emergencies coordination is an obvious and essential part of performing its task and has led WFP to enter into formal and informal agreements with numerous other agencies including NGOs, bilateral donors and private sector enterprises. As early as the era of emergency responses to the 1974 Bangladesh famine, WFP has played a role in coordinating food aid donations from multiple sources. Doing so in the 1990s, especially as part of a UN (or West African) peacekeeping effort, however, poses additional problems and burdens compared to its earlier coordination work in response to natural disasters or market failures. Management of food supplies coming from a variety of locations and funding sources is a daunting task. Different foods in quite different amounts arrive at various harbours, airports and warehouses. To rationally allocate these among various recipients is extremely difficult. Problems are multiplied when relief operations can be halted, hijacked or diverted by local militias. Even in cases of civil conflict in the mid-1980s, for example in Ethiopia, WFP could work with an Ethiopian ministry assisted by the coercive authority of the state. Its efforts to relieve famine occurred in safe conditions with little food stolen. WFP worked inside government regulated areas, leaving bilateral donors and NGOs to assist the Eritreans, Tigrayans and others in rebellion against Mengistu's government. Later, in Mozambique, safety was less available and the number of lost shipments higher, but the WFP/government relationship was maintained. Thus, prior to recent emergencies the principal partners for the World Food Programme have been recipient governments' ministries. Indeed, in its development operations WFP has invariably provided its support as part of a national government effort whether in education, public works, or health. In some countries specific projects have been coordinated with parallel efforts supported by NGOs as practical, for example in India and Egypt. Thus the historic norm for WFP is for its food aid to be coordinated with and facilitated by a government ministry.

In the complex emergencies where peacekeeping is a goal, however, the WFP must deal with a liaison, with military authority and sometimes with rival ones simultaneously, and with a myriad of parallel agencies, each providing various items of emergency relief. Most often this includes the United Nations High Commission for Refugees and the UN Children's Fund. Coordination must be worked out both in the field and among headquarters staff. To facilitate this, WFP has Official Memorandums of Understanding (MOUs) with several UN bodies, including UNHCR and UNICEF.

In addition to such formal memorandums, quite practical understandings exist among staff in the several UN bodies addressing emergencies. Relying on formal and informal norms facilitates cooperation and sharing of expertise in UN field operations. In practice this remains imperfect. WFP also works directly in the field with a number of NGOs. Since 1995 WFP has negotiated formal arrangements with 12 of these bodies. Among NGOs there are important distinctions. The unique ICRC, for example, plays a diffuse role in identifying needs, supplying information and assisting with safe access for convoys. Other NGOs are quite different. They cooperate as parallel and sometimes direct managers of food deliveries. In Angola, for example, CARE, Save the Children and World Vision cooperated with WFP in reaching over 1.8 million people in 1997. In Northern Iraq, WFP provides food while Save the Children oversees a jointly agreed distribution plan. The NGO alliances, however, are fragile since NGOs not only implement on behalf of WFP in failed state situations, but they also compete in Brussels and Washington for resources for projects that they directly seek to manage.

Complex emergencies have created opportunities for leadership by WFP in coordinating food deliveries, usually the most costly resources provided in emergencies. In such cases WFP or a special coordinator for the UN appointed by the Secretary-General normally keeps donor NGOs in daily contact and hosts weekly coordination meetings. Improved coordination among relief, military and political efforts is especially needed when the Security Council approves interventions that violate state sovereignty, as in Somalia and Iraq. Surprisingly, the Northern Iraq episode in 1991, in which military and NGO entities collaborated to rescue Kurdish populations fleeing Republican Guard Troops, worked well thanks to the few agencies involved. Organizational prerogatives were not a concern, as has proved the case in many complex emergencies.[12]

WFP's ability to coordinate is limited by its weak status in the UN system. Hence the creation of a New York-based system-wide coordination office. Nonetheless, WFP remains a subordinate organization to FAO and the United Nations. Ironically the resources it handles are often far more impressive than its authority. This imbalance has made for an especially clumsy situation at times. Military authorities from various nations arriving in Somalia or from West African countries in Liberia have been able to coordinate with WFP largely through other UN agencies since, in the field, WFP is officially under the aegis of the UNDP resident representative, the chief official for WFP in a country.[13]

Logistics

Food is a bulky, perishable commodity. It requires expert management to be successfully transported and stored; many detailed decisions occur when food is moved from an exporting country (or from elsewhere in a recipient country when there is adequate local production) to distribution points. Relief camps are seldom in cities or near goods transportation links. Hence, knowledge of shipping, demurrage, handling, customs, warehousing, inland transport and theft control are necessary. Where complex emergencies exist, frequently local trucking and warehousing firms have disappeared. Thus WFP has to create its own transport and warehouse facilities. These physical resources are costly. In addition, managing them, especially in emergency relief situations in which roads are not only bad but also dangerous, requires skills and training quite different from those that were more central for WFP staff in the earlier stages of its historical evolution. Especially in the 1980s, WFP professional staff training most emphasized increasing knowledge of nutritional assessments and economic development planning.

Compared to other UN agencies and most NGOs, however, WFP has long experience with logistic issues. These management tasks were honed by 30 years of experience by one of the major divisions inside WFP, and skills for these tasks always constituted one area in which regular staff training was provided. Local employees in 'stable' countries, for example, have proved quite valuable as resources for staffing emergency operations elsewhere, utilizing the training, and experience in facilitating logistics developed in their own country. The growth of the WFP after 1975 created much of the need for this capacity in logistical implementation. With increased demands and resources by WFP's member states, logistical capabilities grew in an incremental manner without qualitative changes in status or procedures. Over this period WFP was simply asked to perform expanded tasks within its original development-oriented mandate. Expanding its work in Africa in the 1980s, for example, challenged WFP to deepen its experience in selecting shipping and, when possible, bulk carriers. In addition, contracting for deliveries in remote areas or by aircraft also was mastered. Amounts shipped grew as European states offered their unallocated food aid commodities to WFP for use in Africa; small donors asked WFP to manage the shipment of their bilateral aid to recipients. Staff expansion and redeployment has therefore occurred relatively smoothly according to the requirements of various emergencies. Moreover, as the challenge of delivering emergency assistance grew after 1984, the logistical capacity of WFP responded by delivering more than just food relief to refugees. Often WFP transport resources far outstripped those of other providers to refugee camps, so that WFP was invited to play a diffuse role in moving items. Medicine, shelter and other non-food items have been transported by WFP during UN relief operations. Both in natural emergencies and ones arising from the breakdown of law and order, other UN agencies, notably the UNHCR, have relied on WFP logistics.[14] WFP also moves food into recipient country locations in a contractual relationship with NGOs who are responsible for its actual dispersion to a targeted population.

Thus logistical support has adapted over time and has become an important element that WFP brings to UN coordination in complex emergencies. Liaison among multiple agencies moving emergency supplies has also entailed making sure that no gaps or failures occur in the food distribution network. The movement of provisions in various locations, often provided by a variety of autonomous actors, has required the use of detailed, timely information as well as the sharing of actual transport resources – trucks, trains, draft animals, barges and even porters. The common goal has been adequate provision of people at different locations and at comparable levels of support, so that refugees would not have an incentive to move from one location to another.

A second aspect of the logistical challenge of complex emergency operations has been paying for costly logistics. Since the 1970s, WFP has handled the bulk of its own shipping arrangements; it could even earn cash through its billable shipping services to small bilateral donors. As WFP was drawn into emergency peacekeeping tasks in the 1990s, its logistical experts were in a position to manage the unusual details and unforeseeable crises that invariably attend getting food to difficult locations. Among UN agencies, it had the expertise, information and experience to oversee off-loading, storage and in-country transportation. It was accustomed to doing this with its own vehicles when local private haulers were unavailable. Such logistical experience was often an important advantage that WFP offered to both the NGO community and to UN agencies and governments. Emergency operations, however, entailed a more rapid draw-down of physical resources, such as vehicles. This was the price paid to ensure that food and relief supplies (water, clothing, tents) reached distant areas. With heavy use over treacherous roads, equipment life during emergencies is abnormally short. Without an agency to raise funds and procure and oversee the use of inland transport, however, the management of emergency relief during peacekeeping would be unworkable.

Most logistic management and even some direct emergency costs were funded through regular budget expenditures until the mid-1990s. As WFP shifted responsibilities from development work to emergency or 'rescue' efforts, new formulas for cost recovery in emergencies were devised. Instead of development work subsidizing emergency efforts, a neutral or even reverse funding arrangement was negotiated with key donors.

Insecure Environment

In cases where peacekeeping is underway, not only logistical costs escalate. Lives as well as shipments are at risk. Food must be moved over dangerous terrain if people are to be helped. The conflict, however, may place both UN employees and targeted food aid recipients' lives at greater risk if militia are also hungry or see food as a weapon in their conflict. Consider a recent case in Liberia. In September 1996, 40 displaced Liberians were massacred hours after they received food aid bags. The event prompted others, displaced by the civil war in Liberia, to beg workers to stop bringing them food, as they feared the aid was putting them in even graver danger than the war that drove them from their homes. Even WFP staff in Liberia have become targets of violence.

Such instances have reinforced the notion that UN assistance must be accompanied by physical protection not only for the recipients of the aid but also for those who deliver it to them.[15] WFP inaugurated a military liaison unit in 1996 to facilitate coordination of its rapid response with military officials. This WFP unit, newly approved and staffed by military trained personnel, has the goal of integrating the logistical needs of WFP with military assets.[16] The greater the insecurity, the more the need grows to coordinate food aid deliveries with military operations. David Ramsbotham points out that military guards, anti-kidnap precautions and evacuation plans are all advisable for an agency such as WFP. He states:

> It is becoming increasingly apparent that the field operations of humanitarian Agencies cannot count automatically on their name, or that of the UN to guarantee their security – particularly if they enter a

conflict situation before a UN Mission is firmly established. For example, the situation in the UNHCR refugee camps for Rwandan Hutus in Zaire shows what can happen when a crisis of this scale produces risk and volatility... The point is that preventive humanitarian action is now almost invariably dangerous and must be provisioned accordingly. If there is an accompanying military deployment, the military must be prepared to assist those with humanitarian responsibilities in any way they can.[17]

Organizational Impacts on WFP from Emergency Peacekeeping Operations

In order to improve the provision of emergency feeding, WFP has reorganized. The unit overseeing emergency operations, which had been given autonomy in the 1980s, was integrated back into field operations overseeing country projects. Regional collaboration has been emphasized within operations. The administrations of the Middle East and Latin America regions operations have relocated to their respective regions, while the Asian and African divisions remain at Rome headquarters. In the field, the integration of regular development and emergency operations has shifted management resources out of development. Fewer development projects are being prepared for future commitments. Both headquarters and field staff give high attention to quick emergency response and the management of regional relief. When possible, oversight for an emergency operation is decentralized, as in WFP efforts in Liberia and Sierre Leone.

Conclusion

Studies of the WFP in the early 1990s, noting the broad call at the time for reform of multilateral institutions, proposed ways to streamline development efforts. Discussions within WFP explored prospects for its work to be more closely coordinated with the UNDP or even the World Bank. Bringing development agencies under one umbrella was also a goal entertained by the UN generally, an approach to be coordinated under leadership of an Under-Secretary-General. A decade later, as the century draws to a close, WFP has become more a humanitarian and emergency response agency. Coordination and even consolidation are still issues for WFP in discussions of UN reform, but while still looking to improve efficiency and to increase its coordination with, if not amalgamation into other UN bodies, WFP now has its strongest links with UN and NGO agencies providing relief. This is reflected in formal cooperation arrangements, in the priority of staff to emergency operations, and in the effort to improve liaison with military officials in peacekeeping situations. Such UN reform, if carried to consolidation, would place WFP under the UN in New York, with Humanitarian Affairs overseeing WFP and UNHCR. Reform proposals by academics and by the US government have proposed such schemes. Alternatively, an expanded UNHCR mandate, possibly with WFP playing a supportive role, could also be a consolidation strategy.[18] However much emergency coordination has grown, consolidation seems unlikely while distinct food aid contributions exist within the global aid system.

In this third, current stage of WFP evolution, emergencies have impacted not only the liaison work of WFP but also its intellectual focus. A shift from economic development to social reconstruction is reflected in the language of WFP documents. Child development, family support, nutritional and social outcomes have superseded efficiency and investment in statements of mission policy concerns. These linguistic shifts are underpinned by changes in WFP personnel, their task assignments and patterns of explicit collaboration.

What are the implications of these changes in WFP over the last decade? One is that a debate over the most important mission for food aid, short-term relief or long-term change has been resolved in favour of the former. Emergencies have always taken precedence; now they are the principal function as well. This outcome vindicates the policy preferences of Nordic and other donor countries who have long favoured the exclusive use of food aid for emergencies. Their preferences have now been realized in practice. This outcome is due largely to shifts in the global situation, however, rather than to a triumph of policy analysis. The US, the largest food supplier, abandoned its reluctance to channel emergency food aid multilaterally. The numbers of refugees and internally displaced populations facing starvation without emergency food relief have grown. WFP responded.

A second implication is that short-term immediate problems now dominate the work of WFP. These create a vulnerability. If in future the anarchic conditions that spawned the growth of emergencies and attendant famine threats should subside, WFP is likely to face serious resource contractions. With the tightening of ODA funds generally, arguments that food aid is the second or third best form of development assistance may prevail. Food aid would continue to decline as a share of world food trade. Food security would be a goal justifying agricultural research, improved trade and more humane IMF/World Bank conditionality. WFP would increasingly become an emergency response organization, but an agency with less business. Unlike fire departments, which do not shrink when business is slow (at least not right away), WFP as a food aid deliverer is likely to shrink more noticeably. NGOs face a similar problem. In the 1990s they too have become more often managers of relief operations than overseers of development projects. With fewer longer-term projects aimed at institution-building, human capital formation or infrastructure creation, a reduction in emergency needs will entail a smaller mission and budget. Development activity helped subsidize overhead costs of emergency efforts prior to the 1990s; recently, the reverse has occurred, to a degree. With WFP more dependent for resources that are pledged for short-term emergency work, the organization is more subject to volatile, boom and bust cycles in response to global disasters. As such, its organizational form may evolve to expansion and contraction of peripheral staff, with a smaller professional long-term core.

A final implication of WFP's evolution affects its global policy for the future. The Executive Board and WFP's Executive Director, currently lacking prominence in the UN system, are limited in selecting specific niches for WFP in UN global governance efforts. For example, the coordination of humanitarian efforts during complex emergencies, a task WFP could facilitate, has formally been under the aegis of the DHA. A standing committee (set up in 1992) included such 'big' UN agencies as FAO and WHO, as well as the ICRC, but not WFP. Proposals about humanitarian relief focus often on the UNHCR, UNICEF, and the newly reorganized Office for the Coordination of Humanitarian Affairs (OCHA). Agency roles have all been changing. While the WFP has shifted towards more emergency operations, its companion operations agencies in refugee relief, such as the UNHCR, have grown dramatically. From 1990 to 1996 the UNHCR more than doubled its staff, budget and material resources. As a result, transport and other services, which in the 1980s WFP was primarily equipped to provide in the field, are now available for sharing among agencies under OCHA oversight.[19]

Two options exist as WFP's management plans for the future. In one the WFP could evolve further towards collaboration with and funding of other agencies – primarily NGOs – in humanitarian and emergency work. This would complete the shift from working with national governments to working more directly with recipients. Development objectives would be built into the final phase of emergency work, as now – but without a phase-over to follow-on projects. WFP would be a global manager and broker for donor interests and aligned NGO actions. Possibly it could slowly take over all emergency and food aid functions from donors. This option would need support by OCHA and other UN agencies and it would need to be consistent with the evolving division of labour in the UN system.

The other policy choice for WFP's new role would be for it to increasingly take on the characteristics of an NGO. The ICRC is perhaps a model it could follow, tying together stand-by International Emergency Food Reserve pledges as a resource with an offer of good offices and strict neutrality between or among combating parties in the field. Given its heritage within the UN system, this option would require substantial entrepreneurial effort.

NOTES

1. Data in this essay are from the WFP web site, as of April 1998 (http://www.WFP.org/) and the US Mission to the United Nations, *Global Humanitarianism in Emergencies, 1997*, New York: April 1997.
2. See Mitchel Wallerstein, *Food for War: Food for Peace*, Cambridge: MIT Press, 1980; and Ross Talbott, *The Four World Food Agencies*, Ames, IA: Iowa State University Press, 1990.
3. See Mordecai Ezekiel, *Uses of Agricultural Surpluses to Finance Economic Development in Under-Developed Countries*, 1955, published in volume of reprints, *Food Aid for Development: Three Studies* by Ezekiel, et. al., Rome: FAO, 1985; Vernon Ruttan (ed.), *Why Food Aid?* Baltimore: Johns Hopkins University Press, 1993.
4. See John Shaw and Edward Clay, *World Food Aid*, London: James Currey Ltd., 1993.
5. See Report of the International Wheat Council, London, 1981.
6. Data are from InterFAIS, Rome: WFP, May 1997.
7. 'Food Crops and Shortages', Rome: FAO, February 1998.
8. Andrew Natsios, 'NGOs and the UN System in Complex Humanitarian Emergencies: Conflict or Cooperation?' in Thomas G. Weiss and Leon Gordenker (eds), *NGOs, the UN and Global Governance*, Boulder: Lynne Rienner, 1996, p.68.
9. Reuben P. Mendez, 'Financing the United Nations and the International Public Sector', in *Global Governance*, September–December, 1997, pp.283–9.
10. Complex emergency situations with military elements have led to considerable reflection on new response modalities. See Larry Minear and Thomas G. Weiss, *Mercy Under Fire: War and the Global Humanitarian Community*, Boulder: Westview Press, 1995; Joanna Macrae and Anthony Zwi (eds), *War and Hunger: Rethinking International Responses to Complex Emergencies*, London: Zed Books, 1994; and Michael W. Doyle, Ian Johnstone and Robert C. Orr (eds) *Keeping the Peace: Multidimensional UN Operations in Cambodia and El Salvador*, Cambridge: Cambridge University Press, 1997.
11. Andrew S. Natsios, 'NGOs and the UN System in Complex Humanitarian Emergencies' (see n.8), pp.78–9.
12. Observation of Barnett Baron, Executive Vice-President of Save the Children Foundation, during this period.
13. See Larry Minear and Thomas G. Weiss, *Mercy Under Fire* (see n.10).
14. An accord in 1988 between WFP and UNHCR was worked out by the then Director of the Office of Emergency Operations, Bronek Szynalski, in which WFP, using both its local and international staff, played a central role in providing support services in refugee situations to a variety of donor agencies.
15. US Committee for Refugees, *World Refugee Survey 1997*, p.24.
16. The WFP proposal for ALITE stated: 'In the recent past WFP has made use of military assets in several emergency situations including airlift operations in Ethiopia, Southern Sudan, Somalia, former Yugoslavia and Rwanda, the use of military escorts in Somalia, de-mining and road rehabilitation in Mozambique and Angola, and numerous joint activities with national militaries in a variety of countries... Many militaries in the donor countries, cognizant of this need, have already established humanitarian liaison focal points with which ALITE will establish close working relationships'. (http://wfp.org./)
17. Sir David Ramsbotham, 'Coordination is the Key,' in Jim Whitman and David Pocock (eds), *After Rwanda: The Coordination of United Nations Humanitarian Assistance*, New York: St.

Martin's Press, Inc., 1996, p.121.

18. Carnegie Commission on Preventing Deadly Conflict, *Preventing Deadly Conflict: Final Report*, Washington: Carnegie Commission, 1997, pp.130, 137; and Antonio Donini, 'Asserting Humanitarianism in Peace-Maintenance,' *Global Governance*, January–March 1998, pp.81–96.

19. For example, in 1998 UNHCR vehicles transported WFP food to refugee camps in Tanzania. Further, in Operation Lifeline Sudan (OLS), once a collaborative WFP-UNICEF effort, NGO and UN efforts now operate under OCHA which launches consolidated UN appeals for humanitarian aid needs. Thus, in April 1998, WFP needs for OLS of $31 million were part of a $36 million 'Inter-agency Appeal for Sudan'.

The United Nations Development Programme: The Development of Peace?

DENNIS DIJKZEUL

This article studies the role of the United Nations Development Programme in peacebuilding. First, it examines the overall context in which UNDP operates, in particular the relationship between relief, rehabilitation and development in complex humanitarian emergencies. Second, it investigates UNDP's history, including its gradual move into peacebuilding. Moreover, it reviews UNDP's efforts at organizational renewal, as well as the consequences of current UN reform. Third, the article examines UNDP's need for a more outward and forward looking strategy, focusing on local participation. It presents the conclusion that UNDP has through Sustainable Human Development and its renewal process taken some steps in the right direction, but that this is unfortunately not yet enough to ensure action and results at the field level.

The United Nations Development Programme is a development organization, not a peacekeeping organization. By definition, it did not play a huge role in first-generation peacekeeping, which essentially confined itself to diplomatically engendering a cessation of hostilities and the employment of a neutral, armed observer force.[1] This has changed, in particular since the end of the Cold War. The rapidly rising number of violent conflicts, largely intra-state wars, has led to new forms of peacekeeping. This so-called second-generation peacekeeping encompasses more than just a neutral, military intervention; it also takes on rebuilding war-torn societies in the hope of preventing future conflict. This kind of peacekeeping, generally better seen as rebuilding with an essential security component,[2] by necessity should incorporate a more long-term development perspective. A host of parties – local, (sub-)national, and international – and a wide range of activities – encompassing at the minimum demilitarization, humanitarian and emergency relief, political reconstruction, social reintegration and reconciliation, as well as economic (re)building[3] – interact, and all require urgent, simultaneous action to prevent the recurrence of conflict.[4]

Dennis Dijkzeul is an independent consultant whose main interest is the management of organizations active in rebuilding societies devastated by war.

In principle, UNDP can in its function as a development organization and as a UN coordinating agency play a crucial role in peacebuilding and reconstruction. This article studies whether UNDP plays such a role and asks what the specific difficulties are in performing or attaining it.

UNDP's Context: The Big, Bleak Picture

Many of the factors that constrain or hamper UNDP originate from its environment and its characteristics as a UN organization. The original UN establishment employed a clear division between its security tasks and its development – or broader social and economic – activities. UNDP clearly fell into the development category.

The end of the Cold War was thought to lead to new chances for a more active UN system, and UN involvement in war-torn societies thus grew rapidly. With the benefit of hindsight, one can distinguish four related challenges to which international actors and the UN had to respond. First, neither the international community nor the UN was prepared for action in intra-state wars. There was conceptual confusion and consequent uncertainty as to how to intervene. Second, a specific part of this confusion was addressed in the debate on the difficulties of linking relief, rehabilitation and development in the so-called continuum approach. Third, while the UN system was trying to come to grips with these challenges, the initial post Cold-War confidence in the UN subsided rather quickly. Fourth, the flows of ODA were decreasing.

The wars that erupted after the Cold War presented new, unexpected characteristics that were frequently ill-understood. Their intra-state character made it difficult to determine on which basis international actors could intervene in at least nominally sovereign states. Moreover, UN development cooperation was based on the premise of working with national governments. How to remain neutral in daily practice with the conflicting demands and territorial claims of various parties, varying from local NGOs and local communities to rebel groups, when the government is either absent, weak or illegitimate? What are actually legitimate claims and parties in a situation where the whole societal fabric is breaking down?[5]

Originally, many of the armed conflicts were dealt with primarily from a security perspective. Yet the emphasis on military interventions backfired to a large extent. First, massive military interventions – for example, in Somalia – failed to deliver results. In fact, local coping mechanisms were often destroyed and local needs were insufficiently recognized. Second, development actors were sidelined, while it soon appeared that military actors generally could only play a small role in linking relief, rehabilitation and development.

Much of the debate on conceptualizing the links between relief, rehabilitation and development occurred in the hope of placing these as discrete stages in a continuum.[6] Initially, relief and development activities were carried out by different organizations. This made sense in the wake of natural disasters, in so far as these were one-time events that caused a disruption of regular societal processes but did not destroy the societal fabric. In these cases, relief organizations could usually focus on saving lives through relative short-term operations. This model, in which development could retake its course rather quickly, became the standard model for providing relief during and after conflict.

However, this model soon lost its validity in the growing number of multi-causal complex emergencies that affected the lives and livelihoods of an escalating number of people, mainly located in the developing world.[7] Conventional forms of relief created dependencies: refugee camps became permanent settlements, or they were used as bases for rearmament; food aid negatively affected local food supply and agriculture. Even worse, relief aid was increasingly used by warring factions as a resource in prolonging conflict.[8] Moreover, many of the complex humanitarian emergencies were protracted or recurrent to such an extent that they became semi-permanent. As a result, it became increasingly clear that in many cases short-term conventional relief was hampering long-term development processes by focusing more on the symptoms than on the causes of the disasters.

At the same time, prevention of armed conflict received growing attention. Even in situations of conflict, pockets of stability existed where regular development activities could go on. In other cases, development activities could be integrated into relief, for example by food for work. Although there were great difficulties in getting a war-torn society back on its feet, the aftermath of conflict also offered new possibilities for change. Wood indicates that 'post-conflict situations often provide special opportunities for political, legal, economic, and administrative reforms to change past systems and structures that may have contributed to economic and social inequities and conflict'.[9] Moreover, many initiatives of the local population are carried out independently – if not in spite of – the international donor community. Refugees, for example, have their own means of finding out whether they can safely return, by sending out family members to check the areas of resettlement.[10]

All of this blurs the traditional distinction between security, relief and development. It also implies that rehabilitation has often become the neglected stepchild in the competition between relief and development organizations.[11] In a similar vein, lack of cooperation hinders a coordinated or at least coherent approach towards rebuilding war-torn societies in which short-term relief contributes to longer-term development goals. The traditional categories of security, relief, rehabilitation and development cooperation reflect more the institutional make-up of the international donor-community than the realities at the field level. An armed conflict is a major disruption of development processes, which themselves must already have been dysfunctional by leading up to the conflict.[12] After such a conflict it is rare that the *status quo ex ante* can be re-established on the instigation of external actors. In sum, the assumption that emergencies can be characterized by a continuum going from relief to rehabilitation to development supposes a linear sequence of events through which the original situation can be restored, in part by superimposing external assistance on the local fabric.[13] It thus disregards the simultaneity of development and emergency situations, is 'conceptually wrong' and can be 'operationally misleading'.[14]

As a consequence, relief aid, rehabilitation and development cooperation need to be linked more closely. On the one hand, development should be integrated into relief. On the other hand, regular development activities should also address potential disaster-vulnerabilities and contingencies. In sum, development organizations should prepare themselves for working in crisis environments.

Yet a stronger focus on development does not provide a magic formula, because development cooperation itself has not always been a success story.[15] It is widely felt that development cooperation has too often lacked positive results.[16] To a large extent this has contributed to a donor fatigue that heavily influences the ability of relief and development organizations to function properly. This fatigue was accompanied by the failings in peacekeeping, especially peace enforcement, in countries like Somalia and Rwanda, which caused a precipitous decline in confidence in the capacities of the UN system.

As a result, the UN's resource-base declined. Some broad trends in funding, albeit with irregular counter examples, can be distinguished. The overall amount of ODA has been decreasing. Of this ODA, the amount spent on development cooperation is going down faster than humanitarian relief money.[17] In addition, a considerable amount of funding for development cooperation has been transferred to humanitarian relief and peacekeeping operations. Within funding exclusively for development cooperation, multilateral funding has been decreasing more than bilateral funding. Within multilateral development spending, the amount allocated to the UN is being reduced more quickly than that to the financial institutions. These four factors – lack of preparedness, the conceptual confusion surrounding the continuum debate, dwindling confidence in the UN system and decreasing resources – form the backdrop for UNDP's functioning in complex emergency situations.

The Organization of UNDP

Brief History

In order to understand UNDP's possible contributions to second-generation peacekeeping, it is necessary to get a picture of its regular, development-oriented functioning. Its history and its mission determine the official role that UNDP can play in peacekeeping and peacebuilding.[18]

In 1966, UNDP was set up as a merger between the UN Special Fund and the expanded programme of technical assistance. In particular, the Jackson Report (1969) and the resulting consensus resolution of 1970 – GA resolution 2688 (XXV) – intended UNDP to play a central role in financing and coordinating development cooperation of the UN system. 'UNDP was not given a specific mandate...but simply had as its framework the principles of universality, neutrality, and multilateralism. Its activities were to be based on the recipient countries' own development plans.'[19]

UNDP was supposed to become a funding organization with a large field presence, where the UNDP Country Director – officially called the Resident Representative, or briefly the Res Rep – would always be designated as the Resident Coordinator of the UN field presence. This Res Rep would thus wear two hats: the UNDP leadership and the official coordinator of all other UN organizations. To this end UNDP, both at headquarters and in the field, also carried out administrative and supportive functions for the other UN organizations, especially for those belonging to the UN proper, such as UNFPA.

UNDP operated within the tripartite system of UN development cooperation, which involves a funding agency, an executing agency and a coordinating agency. As a funding agency, UNDP provides the funds and assists the country government, which is the coordinating agency, with the planning and management of its development programmes. The government officially requests and approves the development programmes. Traditionally, the executing agencies are most often the specialized agencies. They generally provide the technical inputs in development cooperation, such as training courses, technical experts and specialized equipment.[20] At present, UNDP increasingly promotes national execution, for example with subnational governments and local NGOs.

Through the Resident Coordinator system and its funding position, it was hoped that UNDP could effectively carry out its coordination tasks. Moreover, the fact that it was not given a specific mandate would allow UNDP to pick up the slack from other UN organizations. If in a specific country a certain area of development was not being covered by a UN organization, UNDP was allowed to jump in. This would, it was hoped, once again strengthen its coordinating role and ensure a balanced multi-sectoral development process at the country level.

Unfortunately, for UNDP and UN coordination, other UN organizations were able to defy UNDP's central role in funding. In particular the specialized agencies, who are only loosely coupled to the UN proper by mutual agreements and have their own decision-making bodies, have been able to find other resources from donor governments and to strengthen their independence. The donor governments never gave enough money to UNDP to allow its coordinating role as central-funding institute to materialize.[21]

For about 20 years, the specialized agencies had another bone to pick with UNDP. As an outcome of the consensus resolution, UNDP set up its own executing arm: the Office for Project Services.[22] From then on, the agencies complained that UNDP, as a funding organization, had become both judge and jury in assigning projects for execution. UNDP in return maintained that the executing work of OPS covered specific areas not covered by other agencies and that its work was generally of a management support nature – that is, administrative tasks and consultancies. In 1995, after pressure from Secretary-General Boutros Ghali who ostensibly considered that OPS hampered UNDP's coordinating role, OPS became an independent UN body as the United Nations Office for Project Services.[23] UNOPS is responsible to UNDP's Executive Board, and UNDP's administrator has a seat in its management committee. Surprisingly, UNDP is currently engaged in a pilot phase of once again setting up its own executing arm under the heading of promoting national execution. UN organizations seem to have a great propensity for reinventing the wheel.[24] For UNOPS this means that the old parent organization is becoming a competitor, whose administrator simultaneously oversees UNOPS's management. The relationship between UNDP and UNOPS obviously requires further clarification.

In the 1980s, UNDP came under fire for its activities not being focused enough, so that it was spreading itself too thinly. In 1994, the Executive Board of UNDP decided that the organization's future activities should take place within the framework of the Sustainable Human Development (SHD) concept.[25] Through its annual human development reports, UNDP has played a pivotal role in developing and promoting this concept. SHD was a major countervailing power against the structural adjustment programmes from the Bretton Woods institutions, which originally paid far too little attention to the social sustainability of their one-sided macro-economic programmes. The SHD concept has become one of UNDP's recent success stories, gaining increasing currency after the Social Summit from 1995. UNDP now considers as its mission: assistance to countries in their efforts to achieve sustainable human development by helping them to build their capacity to design and carry out development programmes in poverty eradication, employment creation, and sustainable livelihoods, the empowerment of women, and the protection and regeneration of the environment, giving first priority to poverty eradication.[26]

Complementary to its mission, UNDP employs two other overriding goals:

• To help the UN become a powerful and cohesive force for sustainable human development.

• To strengthen international cooperation for sustainable human development and serve as a major substantive resource on how to achieve it.

In this way, UNDP has attempted to carve out a specialized and substantive niche where it can be seen as the central UN agency, comparable for example to UNFPA in the population field. The question then becomes: how specialized and substantive is SHD? In this respect, UNDP is being criticized that it 'has not yet specified how it will operationalize SHD. Nor has the organization formulated a strategy for the implementation of SHD or been able to define its task within the broad framework of SHD, including which tasks it will perform in which areas and, conversely, which tasks it will refrain from performing'.[27] So the criticism of a lack of focus returns, albeit in a more specific way.

A related facet of growing criticism of UNDP centres on its relationship with governments. Donors express concern about the overbearing role of the recipient country governments that is said to lead UNDP away from its own priorities.[28] (Yet these critics fail to realize that UNDP was supposed to be government-oriented, multi-sectoral and country-specific.) UNDP is also criticized for paying insufficient attention to local communities and other non-governmental actors. UNDP partly addressed this criticism by promoting sub-national and NGO execution, which would also facilitate local capacity building. It has also responded to this criticism by setting up area-based projects, which for example can focus on local pockets of poverty in an integrated manner. UNDP considers itself one of the pioneers of this form of programming. Nevertheless, UNDP was set up to be responsive to the desires of sovereign country governments, so what can it do if a government pays insufficient heed to parts of its population? In difficult countries, such as North Korea and Rwanda, because of its involvement UNDP can sometimes play a low-key advocacy role and offer alternatives, but in comparison to many NGOs it pays for its governmental access with a smaller space in which to manoeuvre freely.

In 1994, UNDP's coordinating role for the UN system received a boost when the Secretary-General Boutros Ghali entrusted Gus Speth, the UNDP Administrator, with the 'responsibility for assisting him in improving the coordination of operational activities, including the strengthening of the resident coordinator system'.[29] In this way, one of the central roles of the Administrator was moved closer to that of the Secretariat, which demonstrates one of the fundamental ambiguities – some say schizophrenia – of UNDP: does it primarily take care of its own activities or does it pay more attention to UN coordination? In particular, the Res Reps are confronted with the internal dilemmas and agency complaints that come with this ambivalence.

Currently, UNDP has a network of 132 offices world-wide and it works with 174 governments. The wide field presence and UNDP's multi-sectoral perspective can also be seen as comparative advantages. As a result of its long presence in the field and government access, UNDP can build up intimate local knowledge and relationships throughout a country, which are not available to other organizations or relief actors. As a UN organization, it is in many countries also seen as a neutral broker. In principle, UNDP is thus uniquely positioned to develop and advocate a holistic, long-term development perspective.[30] This can also facilitate UN in-country coordination. Here, much depends on the personal qualities of the Res Rep. It is not an easy task to make the comparative advantages work.[31] Consequently, these advantages constitute more in the way of potentials than actual achievements.[32]

In sum, UNDP has incrementally been changing its roles. Whereas in the 1970s, it was more of a technical agency, nowadays it is becoming a knowledge centre and an agent for advocacy. Managerially, it is still vulnerable to criticism that it is spreading itself too thinly, although it is increasingly trying to focus itself through SHD. This leads to a fundamental tension: on the one hand, UNDP has to remain true to its original conception as a central, multi-sectoral and country-specific agency; and on the other, it is under pressure to focus itself more. Its coordinating role and wide field presence can present both difficulties and opportunities in this respect. In addition, most criticism centres on the insufficient operationalization of sustainable human development and the government focus. UNDP has taken some steps in the right direction, but SHD is not coherent and implementable enough yet. In other words, UNDP needs to show better that it is action-oriented and can deliver results at field level.

Preparing the Ground: Setting Up ERD

In principle, the basic tenets of SHD tally well with the need for strengthening local capacities for rebuilding. In the early nineties, UNDP staff struggled with its role in conflict situations and noticed that as a development organization, UNDP could play a role in preventing and resolving conflict. At the field level, it became clear that with the conflict situations after the Cold

War the distinction between security, relief, and development was no longer tenable. Moreover, UNDP staff received growing criticism from NGO and ICRC staff that it was packing its suitcases too soon when conflict broke out. At the same time other actors, in particular those concerned with relief, did not appreciate a greater role for UNDP. In many cases, UNDP was sidelined when the Secretary-General appointed Special Representatives of the Secretary-General (SRSG) in crisis situations. These SRSGs were supposed to coordinate, and thus took over UNDP's regular role. UNDP could at best become a supporting act.

So whereas it was logical to assume that UNDP could contribute to a broad, long-term development perspective, UNDP was a relative latecomer who was not received with open arms. As a consequence, it first had do its own homework for this sort of action. In 1992, UNDP officials decided to respond to the new wave of crises, but they still had to convince the Executive Board. In essence, they thought that UNDP country offices should address volatility instead of shutting down. To be able to do this, the field offices needed access to more flexible money. The organizational structure and policies would then also require revision.

In the period from 1992 to 1996, the thinking within UNDP slowly changed. The regional bureaux were relatively slow in picking up the necessary changes. In 1992, the Executive Board approved more attention to humanitarian operations. In 1994, the Emergency Response Division (ERD) was created. It was part of the UNDP's Office of the United Nations System Support and Services within the Office of the Administrator, which shows how closely ERD was going to be related to UNDP's coordinating tasks. Only ten people work at ERD, two of whom are located in Geneva – remarkably few for such an enormous task.

UNDP categorizes its own tasks in emergencies into four groups, which mirror UNDP's general coordinating and funding work, including picking up the slack in the larger UN system. The groups cover the whole range of pre-crisis, crisis, and post-crisis activities, for both natural and man-made disasters:[33]

1. Carrying out activities of a semi-emergency character, with extra-budgetary funds provided by one or several donors (including funds from UN assessed budgets), when these activities do not fall within the mandate of a particular UN entity.
2. Identifying the elements of an overall strategy or programme framework for national and international action, whether in conjunction with the consolidated inter-agency appeals launched by DHA, through Round Tables or Special Consultations, or through ad hoc programming missions.

3. Financing specific activities, of a preventive and curative nature, from general resources or special accounts under UNDP's control, using other UN agencies and organizations of civil society as implementing partners.
4. In-country coordination of programme implementation through the resident coordinator's office, providing administrative support services for the donor community.

UNDP also commissioned studies to examine its strengths, weaknesses and opportunities in crisis-situations. Not uncommon in bureaucracies, one study that proposed a number of bold UNDP reforms, was not taken up.[34] In all likelihood, some personnel changes and the increasing strains in the relationship with DHA required a more immediate response. For DHA also had a coordinating role for the UN system in emergencies. DHA could have been a natural ally, but instead, as so often in the UN system, a more competitive relationship evolved. UNDP therefore created an inventory of its activities in emergencies for DHA, the other UN organizations and outsiders as a compendium of its record in crisis countries.[35] The following scheme shows UNDP's compendium and the main cooperating partners.

DHA and UNDP also worked together on disaster preparedness in the Disaster Management Training Programme, which through workshops brings together the UN system and other national and international development and relief organizations. 'The subject of follow-up to emergencies, and the need to consider and plan for the longer-term reintegration and rehabilitation implications is an essential part of this training.'[36] In most countries, the workshop is followed up with the establishment of a United Nations Disaster Management Team (DMT).[37] In sudden disasters and other non-complex emergencies, such as storms and floods, the Resident Representatives (Res Rep) Coordinator and the DMT form the first group to act. With emergencies that are more extended and complex, such as slow-onset natural disasters (for example, drought) and most man-made disasters, the Res Rep and the DMT often move to the background, because the SRSG, humanitarian coordinator and other actors start playing a more dominant role. As Table 1 indicates, DHA and UNDP also work together in formulating consolidated interagency appeals.

UNDP's operational experience shows that it has once again cast its net widely. It thus has to cooperate with many other organizations. In principle, this can provide UNDP's work with a broad scope without wasting too many resources on opportunity costs for maintaining stand-by capacity. Nevertheless, it is not clear whether UNDP has any comparative advantage in these areas of activity, nor does a compendium show the specific capacities UNDP possesses or what its priorities are. In particular, the

TABLE 1
UNDP RECORD IN CRISIS COUNTRIES

1. Emergency Interventions *Key operating partners:* DHA, UNHCR, WFP, UNICEF, WHO, FAO, EU, Bilateral Donors, NGOs	a) Resources for disaster assessments b) Crisis management and support for relief delivery c) Support for program activities
2. Programming for Peace and Recovery *Key operating partners:* DHA, UNHCR, WFP, UNICEF, Specialized Agencies, World Bank, IMF, EU	a) Participation in consolidated inter-agency appeals b) Organizations of special consultations or round tables c) Ad hoc programming missions d) Monitoring of aid flows e) Establishment of early warning systems f) National long term perspectives g) Development mapping of districts and regions
3. Area Rehabilitation to Resettle Uprooted Populations *Key operating partners:* UNOPS, UNHCR, WFP, UNEP, HABITAT, UNCDF, UNIFEM, Specialized Agencies, EU, Bilateral Donors, IFIs, NGOs	a) Resettlement and reintegration of displaced people b) Restoration of health and education services c) Rebuilding infrastructure and production systems d) Local planning and participatory mechanisms e) Environmental rehabilitation
4. Reintegrating Demobilized Soldiers *Key operating partners:* DPKO, ILO, WHO, World Bank, UNV, UNOPS, IOM	a) Operational support during cantonment b) Organization of severance pay and other aid packages c) Matching job and training opportunities with demand d) Organization of credit schemes for self-employment
5. Demining *Key operating partners:* DPKO, DHA, UNOPS, EU, Bilateral Donors, NGOs, NPA, MAG, Halo Trust, HI	a) Operational and institutional support b) Mine prevalence surveys and database
6. Rebuilding Institutions and Improving Governance *Key operating partners:* DPA, UNCHR, World Bank, Regional IFIs, Bilateral Donors	a) Analysis of civil reform needs b) Coordination of capacity-building programs c) Decentralization and local government d) Observance of human rights e) Land reform and regulation of land tenure
7. Organizing National Elections *Key operating partners:* DPA, UNV, International Institute for Democracy and Electoral Assistance, Bilateral Donors, EU	a) Training in election procedures and logistics b) Voter registration and supervision of polling c) Organization of observer presence
8. Managing Delivery of Programme Aid *Key operating partners:* UNOPS, Bilateral Donors, World Bank, Regional IFIs	a) Monitoring and supervision of commodity aid b) Procurement of imports

Source: UNDP Record in Crisis Countries

strategic linkages to SHD and its operationalization for emergencies can be worked out further, for example with regard to prevention and good governance.

To its credit, UNDP has tried to build up its financial and programming capacity and flexibility. In 1995, the Executive Board decided on programming arrangements allocating five per cent of UNDP's core resources to development in countries facing special situations. This US$ 50,000,000 is called TRAC 3 (Target for Resource Assignment from the Core) money. This is essentially a budget line for programming that 'permits UNDP to respond more quickly to these situations. These resources are meant to be used in a catalytic manner to mobilize complementary financial and in-kind resources to those of other development partners'.[38] To this end, TRAC 3 money is primarily the responsibility of the Res Reps, who do not need government approval as with other projects. It covers three categories of funding, represented in Table 2.

TABLE 2
UNDP TRAC 3 ALLOCATION

Category	Allocated Amount in US$ 50,000,000
1. Program responses to complex development situations, during crisis and post-crisis, including:	
a) strategic frameworks for international/national action	35,000,000
b) special program initiatives within such frameworks	5,000,000
2. Immediate support to strength the country/UN system's ability to provide a coordinated, urgent response to sudden crisis	5,000,000 each allocation (up to) 200,000
3. Capacity-building to avoid and prepare for crises:	
a) training (awareness and HRD)	2,000,000
b) programs for crises-management	7,000,000
c) capacity-building (backstopping Res Coordinator/Res Reps for planning and coordination)	1,000,000

Source: UNDP TRAC 3 Allocation.

In its allocation of TRAC 3 funding, UNDP departs from the premise that it is going to cooperate with other organizations. It also attempts to strengthen in-country UN coordination. Yet this is not always appreciated by other organizations. Through its TRAC 3 resources UNDP tried to be pro-active in promoting the strategic framework, a concept which is currently being developed. On the basis of experience in countries such as Somalia and

Mozambique, UN staff, especially SRSGs, had become aware of the need for political action to end conflict as well as a joint vision both to reassess individual organizations' strategies and resolve the tension between short-term action and long-term needs. This need is especially poignant when there is no central government and there are many NGOs, UN organizations and donors present. The strategic framework was supposed to address this need and to be a joint tool that goes further than the regular consolidated appeals. Yet CCPOQ, DHA and DPA were also involved in creating this instrument. Since the strategic framework was, and remains, not fully developed, these and other organizations perceived that by creating its TRAC 3 guidelines, UNDP was hijacking the instrument.

Internally, there was confusion over whether all countries should be allowed to formulate a strategic framework or whether only designated crisis countries could. In the end, all countries were given permission, and Res Reps took the initiative to formulate such frameworks (with the additional advantage that this meant more money for 'their' country office), but this increased confusion with other organizations, who thought that the strategic framework still needed to be elaborated and pilot tested in cooperation with them. In response, UNDP renamed the in-country strategic frameworks 'programme outlines' and thus moved them closer to the regular programming process.

Currently, it is still not clear whether the strategic frameworks idea will become a useful tool. It is still under development and is therewith part of the political games among UN organizations. But whatever the future may bring, the strategic framework shows a fundamental dilemma of UNDP coordination: if UNDP is too pro-active, other organizations will accuse it of hijacking activities; if UNDP 'waits and sees' what other organizations will do, it is perceived as doing too little. Everybody will assert that UN coordination is necessary, but when push comes to shove they will only consent to the process on their own terms. UNDP often lacks the resources and clout to overcome these obstacles.

In sum, UNDP's first steps into emergencies were not the consequence of a carefully planned strategy. Formulating a compendium is only a small step, because it does not describe the organization's strengths and weaknesses, nor does it clarify its strategic priorities. TRAC 3 funding is already moving in the direction of a more structured response. Positively formulated, UNDP emergency activities were clear examples of incrementalism; negatively formulated, they were examples of muddling through while trying to protect its role and scramble for resources. In this regard, Moore states about UN organizations:

Development entities should resist chasing emergency roles as a way of getting a higher profile or attracting more funds. Everyone should concentrate more on building a capacity to get the job done better rather than to secure an advance guarantee of certain piece of the action, especially UNDP.[39]

It is exactly internal capacity building on which UNDP can focus without interference from other UN organizations. At present, the links between SHD and emergencies need to be clarified further and some critical questions remain: although UNDP has attempted to build up its own capacity, it is not clear whether this has been done successfully and whether it has gained credibility with other organizations. Is UNDP geared for action? Is it able to address the root causes of conflict as they relate to underdevelopment, poverty and inequities? How does it integrate SHD into peacebuilding? Frequently, UNDP has to work with partners that carefully safeguard their influence and independence. How does this influence UNDP's functioning? An evaluation of its TRAC 3 activities can help to shed some light on these critical issues.

The UNDP Renewal?

While UNDP was setting up ERD, the whole organization came under increasing strain. UNDP had attempted to focus itself, but now the organization felt it risked losing relevance in the fight against poverty and that it would become marginalized.[40] A major overhaul was needed, because of six trends:[41]

1. In development cooperation, the 'age of entitlement' has ended. Donors no longer support the concept of blanket resource transfers. They seek focus, efficiency and results. Donors increasingly earmark resources for specific projects.
2. In real terms, the 1995 levels of ODA are almost the same as in 1985. The share going to multilateral agencies is down, and within that share UNDP's portion has waned from eight per cent in 1982 to five per cent in 1995. From 1990 to 1996, UNDP had to cut staff and costs three times. It also had to cut programme funds. In 1996, the US cut its contribution by 54 per cent, which was a great loss for UNDP. The resource bases of UNDP have also become more diversified: co-financing through donor trust funds and third-party contributions account for about half of UNDP's income.
3. The number of poor people is still growing. A new and more inclusive framework for development cooperation with regard to poverty eradication is urgently needed.
4. The market for development services is crowded, with more – and

sometimes more efficient – contenders, such as public, private, academic and technical agencies, as well as NGOs, competing for shrinking resources.

5. In many quarters, the image of the UN is unfavourable. A reputation for inefficiency plagues the world body. Perhaps even more fundamentally, the legitimacy and role of development assistance is being questioned.

6. Requests from programme countries are more diverse and demanding. Technical cooperation needs are now highly divergent, with middle-income countries able to finance services themselves and low-income and least-developed nations still struggling to acquire basic capacities. A global agency must provide differentiated, targeted and competitive services on a wide and uneven front.

Moreover, within UNDP some staff acknowledged that the organization is not as efficient as it should be in delivering the resources it has. Staff have also felt a need for streamlining procedures for programming and budgeting, as well as for better relationships between headquarters and country offices. For example, SHD policy formulation and practical SHD field experience coexisted without very little interaction. This coincides with the older trend that UNDP's central role in development has insufficiently materialized. And as the consensus resolution of 1970 was becoming outdated as a model for development cooperation, UNDP's basic structure and methods had not changed during those decades.[42]

In response, UNDP initiated a change process called UNDP 2001 that was supposed to be pro-active in positioning and strengthening UNDP. One of the main professed goals of UNDP 2001 is to reverse the organizational retreat and embark on a strategy for growth.[43] To indicate that this was not intended to be a piecemeal improvement, UNDP preferred to speak of renewal instead of reform.

UNDP installed a Change Management Committee that was to oversee the project team 'UNDP 2001'. The project team guided and facilitated a vision on the future of UNDP. It worked with seven project groups, which each studied a thematic area in more detail and came up with recommendations. These project groups were:

1. Funding and Strategic Partnerships, in which the opportunities and conditions for resource mobilization and linking up with other parties played an important role.

2. Strategic Development Services, which concentrated on UNDP's client focus and competencies.

3. Efficiency, Accountability and Results Orientation, which covered a wide range of topics varying from performance measurement to shared values and a code of ethics.

4. Structure and Management, which reviewed the distribution of tasks between Headquarters and country offices and the collaboration between the different organizational units in the light of possible decentralization.
5. Human Resources Management, which studied and made recommendations on managing the workforce and developing staff and organizational capabilities, as well as the role of human resources management in making the organization more results-oriented.
6. Information Management and Communications, which investigated how information management and communications infrastructure could enable UNDP reform and performance.
7. External Communications and Public Affairs, which examined the constraints, opportunities and achievements of UNDP's communication and public affairs activities.

These groups provided a wealth of recommendations for transforming UNDP. Many of these were approved by the Executive Board in May 1997. One of the problems that UNDP had to confront was that it had to keep on board both its personnel and its member states. In the end, some felt that consultations with the member states had been necessary to harness political support, but that it delayed and frustrated staff involvement.

Implementation was planned in three partly overlapping phases: launch, restructuring and consolidation. The launch phase lasted from May until the end of August 1997:

- During this phase a new Bureau for Planning and Resource Management was set up. It is supposed to help headquarters refocus on strategic issues, instead of operational action. BPRM will support senior management decision-making and must link planning, budgeting, programme resource allocation and personnel assignment more closely.
- A new Operations Support Unit was set up with the purpose of supporting the Associate Administrator. ERD became part of OSU and was thus separated from OUNS and its role in supporting the Resident Coordinator system.
- The UNDP plan and budget for 1998 and 1999 were integrated to take into account the change initiatives.
- An efficiency ombudsperson was appointed.
- Early actions that can show quick results were also initiated. UNDP field offices and headquarters now work with a five-day response time to speed up action. Regional Bureaux employ a one-stop shop for country offices, which should facilitate cutting reporting requirements from country offices. Finally, a Better Meetings Programme was installed to improve quality and output of UNDP meetings.

The restructuring phase took place from July to the end of 1997. In this period:

* Headquarters units were restructured and new responsibilities were incorporated to support decentralization, so that Headquarters will concentrate on planning, advocacy, accountability and fundraising. It was hoped that as a result, UNDP would become a flatter organization.
* UNDP established a system of sub-regional facilities (SURFs) in the five programme regions it serves. These will be linked across regions and to UNDP headquarters in New York. Drawing on international, regional and national agencies and experts, the facilities will identify the best expertise for development programmes and capture and disseminate the lessons learned. In short, the SURFs take care of expertise referral and backstopping. Hence, they are meant to help UNDP become a learning organization.[44]
* To further decentralization, full authority has been delegated to UNDP country offices to develop and approve programmes within the country cooperation framework. The latter needs to be authorized by the Executive Board. In this regard, there are now two-way compacts between regional bureaux and country offices. On the one hand, these compacts identify the goals, targets and required support for the country offices, on the other they provide the basis for the oversight functions of the regional bureaux.
* Measures were taken to strengthen OUNS (which was renamed Office of the UN Development Group). Staff from other UN bodies is seconded and the administrator oversees the Resident Coordinator system. In this way, UNDP is giving increasing priority to UN coordination.

The consolidation phase is currently taking place and will last until the end of 1999. As its name implies, this phase aims to strengthen and solidify the change process. In the consolidation phase, the emphasis is on decentralization by simplifying and improving procedures and rotating or moving out staff.

* Five to ten additional SURFs will be established and a SURF hub will be located in the Policy Bureau.
* UNDP's manuals will be simplified and distributed in hard copies and on CD-ROM in the hope of reducing bureaucratic paperwork and speeding up the workflow.
* Management and performance indicators will be developed to further operationalize the oversight function of the Regional Bureaux.
* The redeployment of staff and posts to Country Offices and SURFs, which had already started in the restructuring phase, will be completed.

This means that about 20 per cent of headquarters professional staff will move out to the field in a period of three years.

In principle, these changes can indeed drive a renewal of UNDP. They combine decentralization, resource mobilization and accountability in the hope of creating a more effective learning organization. In themselves, these measures make sense. They contribute to a more business-like UNDP. Nevertheless, UNDP does not operate in a business-like environment. As so often in the UN, the ideas are sound, but can they be operationalized so that implementation runs smoothly?

With regard to UNDP's attempt to incorporate business-like management techniques, it is disturbing that UNDP 2001 has to a large extent been inward looking. The focus of the seven working groups has been mainly on UNDP itself. An eighth working group on external environment scanning was not continued as a separate endeavour. Hence, the changes in the environment of the organization have been mentioned, but the implications for the substance of UNDP's functioning have been insufficiently studied.[45]

This lack of attention can create two strategic drawbacks for the reform process: the role of governments *vis-à-vis* the other societal actors and the relationships among development, complex emergencies and peacebuilding both deserve more strategic attention.

In line with modern management assumptions, UNDP has tried to become more client-centred. Yet the question is whether one can easily 'pick' the 'right' client in a public task like multilateral development cooperation. UNDP considers the country government (or its decision-makers) its primary client, because it 'can exert maximum leverage to impact on the lives of the poorest and most vulnerable groups'.[46] UNDP's governmental focus may be in line with the traditional set-up of the UN system, which was based on the concept of sovereignty, but it is also being criticized. In the context of SHD, it is crucial to ask whether it is the government or the poor themselves who have most leverage in alleviating poverty.

Of course, the government is necessary, but it is only the poor who can make action sustainable. In all likelihood, a more balanced view on the role of government is necessary. This is also important in terms of national execution and the traditional tripartite system. There is no general way to determine why and when the central government, local authorities, UNOPS, UNDP's new executing arm, other UN organizations or NGOs should become the executing agent of UNDP-funded activities. In this context, the question may once again be how to work closer with local communities and let them determine who is going to execute what. Otherwise, development cooperation can either lack results or create dependencies. The questions pertaining to UNDP's relationship with governments are even more starkly posed during emergencies. In many crisis countries a central government does not even exist, or its legitimacy is generally disputed. Moreover, war quickly destroys the benefits of an SHD approach. Here, working with local communities in a participatory fashion to indiginize development cooperation becomes even more crucial.[47] Capacity building in war-torn societies can subsequently imply setting up and strengthening government services, but only later on in the process of recovery is it likely that the government can become the primary client.[48]

Internally, the lack of attention to UNDP's environment and specifically to complex emergencies is shown by an almost total absence of a discussion on the role of ERD.[49] Its exact role in OSU is not clear yet. Moreover, ERD is now separated from OUNS. Yet the relationship of ERD with this office needs clarification, because ERD is supposed to help Resident Coordinators in emergency situations. In a similar vein, the relationship between ERD and the regional bureaux requires more attention. ERD has to operate in a cross-sectoral manner, but how is its relationship with more regular, regionally-based development activities defined? In this respect, there is confusion within UNDP over what should happen with non-TRAC 3 money in emergency countries without a central government, such as Somalia. Does ERD possess responsibility in this regard or can it only focus on TRAC 3 activities?

UNDP's change process has been an encompassing exercise that has to be evaluated for impact, but in many ways first the dust has to settle. However, the change process cannot be called a complete overhaul or renewal: it needs to be supplemented with more attention to changes in its environment and the implications for the substance of its work, in particular in the light of the need for more bottom-up, local participation. For example, UNDP could develop a strategy for linking development, complex emergencies and peacebuilding, indicating UNDP's priorities. This would in all likelihood imply changes in modes of execution. It would also provide inputs for an internal discussion on the role of ERD, which needs to be clarified. All in all, UNDP is heading in the right direction, but it cannot show yet whether it has the capacity to implement its mission. Despite the renewal, it remains uncertain whether UNDP is geared to action in such a way that it can deliver results at the field level.

UNDP and UN Reform

UNDP is not alone in its changes. Reform has become a fashionable activity throughout the whole UN system. Frequently, similar reasons are mentioned to initiate comparable processes of change. In 1997, Secretary-General Kofi

Annan initiated a UN wide reform process.[50] Briefly, his proposals focused mainly on the structure of the UN system and became very much a top-down exercise with the informal purpose of appeasing major donors. Although many of the proposals have their merits, the changes in the environment and the implications for the substance of the UN system's work received scant attention.[51] For example, the crucial question of how the UN development cooperation can become more participatory was not really taken up. It appears that reform of both UNDP and the larger UN are at least coordinated in sharing a similar shortcoming.

A central element in UN reform relating to peacebuilding concerns the Department of Humanitarian Affairs, which has been scaled down and transformed into the Office of the Coordinator for Humanitarian Assistance (OCHA). To a large extent this is because DHA had become more operational and was perceived as a threat by other UN organizations. DHA also possessed a coordinating role, which created an ambivalent relationship with UNDP. The discussion on reforming DHA was insufficiently based on what the UN system can do to relieve suffering and to integrate relief with rehabilitation and development. The following points indicate the main planned consequences of DHA's reform for UNDP:

1. UNDP will take over prevention, preparedness and mitigation of natural disasters. The modalities for the transfer are now being worked out. For ERD, this means a reshuffling of its priorities now that natural disasters will form a larger share of the budget. There are similarities between man-made and natural disasters. From an organizational perspective, both types of disasters require flexible procedures and funding policies, rapid responses and adaptive mainstream policies – for example, focusing on reducing vulnerability and stressing preparedness. Still, experience has also shown the limited applicability of the continuum approach for complex emergencies.

2. UNDP also works on demining. Demining is an important condition for facilitating long-term development. The Department of Peacekeeping Operations (DPKO) will take over the demining responsibilities from DHA. As a consequence, UNDP will have to work closely with DPKO in this area.

3. UNDP will continue working in the Inter-Agency Standing Committee (IASC) which also includes major NGOs. The IASC advises on the need for a Humanitarian Coordinator and endorses the selection of these coordinators. However, the distinction between the Humanitarian Coordinator and the Resident Coordinator will be abolished. In the past, these two had to function side by side. 'The Resident Coordinator will now represent the entire UN system, although where there is also a

humanitarian coordination function, the Coordinator would report to both UNDP and OCHA.'[52]

4. The newly-established Executive Committee for Humanitarian Affairs (ECHA) will be chaired by OCHA. UNDP is represented in ECHA, which further consists of the relief organizations, DPA and DPKO. As a result, UNDP is more involved in political discussions and will become more visible in humanitarian emergencies.

5. The Department of Political Affairs (DPA) will act as chair and secretariat of the Executive Committee on Peace and Security. This Executive Committee has been appointed the focal point for the UN in post-conflict peacebuilding. In all likelihood, DPA will be responsible for the development and implementation of the strategic frameworks. As a result, DPA will become one of ERD's main partners.[53]

6. Finally, the UN Development Group will be established. UNDP's OUNS, renamed as the Office for the UN Development Group, will become the secretariat for this Group, and the UNDP administrator will act as chair. Once again, UNDP is in a position where it will have to answer the question: what will come first, UNDP's self-interests or the coordination of the UN system? It is hard to prejudge the outcomes of the Development Group. UNICEF has lobbied against the installation of this Development Group.[54] At first glance, it appears that UNDP's coordinating role has been strengthened, but the reform proposal states that the respective mandates of the organizations need to be respected. In other words, the organizations can safeguard their independence, which has been the regular kiss of death to all UN coordination efforts.

Apparently, UN reform has not weakened UNDP's position. The informal competition with DHA has disappeared, and UNDP has received new tasks in the fields of natural disasters and new challenges in coordination.

Future Directions?

In many ways it is still too early to assess the results of the UN reform and its own change process for UNDP. Much will depend on the cooperation of member states, in particular on their willingness to contribute financially and to synchronize their policies. Past experience does not provide ground for excessive optimism. The focus of the reforms on structural change shows how limited the reform proposals actually are.

A fundamental discussion is needed on the role of both the international donor community and UNDP and their possible contributions to relief, rehabilitation and development. UNDP is not alone in this respect. The whole international aid community is grappling with the problems raised by peacekeeping and underdevelopment, in particular in relationship to local participation. Reactions vary from taking a cynical distance, to a feeling of doom and gloom, to a slow, sometimes painful, search for new solutions in policy-making and organizational implementation. Unhappily, these often remain at the level of rhetoric and are insufficiently translated into action at the field level.

The main general strategic question for UNDP will be: how to operationalize SHD, in general and for peacebuilding in particular? This involves further study of modes of execution and the role of the governments in order to use more participatory approaches. Development cooperation displays fundamental paradoxes in this respect. Bringing in outside resources in order to promote local self-reliance is contradictory. Development cooperation seeks to influence the behaviour of people, and it is therefore always dependent on these people. Seen from this perspective, dependency is a two-way street. In addition, since UN organizations are set up to work with governments: what to do when governments do not govern properly? Despite all the rhetoric, it rarely happens that the local actors are fully involved – let alone in 'self reliant' control – in all stages of development programmes. The concept of SHD offers incentives for involving the grassroots level, and UNDP has done so through such initiatives as area-based projects. Unfortunately, the inward-looking focus of the renewal process does not concentrate enough attention on these issues.

More specifically, UNDP should assess the changing characteristics of violent conflicts. First, many of the post Cold War conflicts are now moving into the post-conflict stage, where more regular UNDP development is required. Second, new conflicts that will erupt will frequently result from the combined forces of overpopulation, environmental degradation and economic marginalization, even though at first they may appear to be ethnic or religious conflicts. Hence the development aspects of these conflicts require careful consideration. An actor like UNDP can play a useful role in both coordination and programming in all stages of such conflicts.

In addition to these general questions, this article has also highlighted UNDP-specific factors that hamper its ability to perform successfully in peacebuilding. The following scheme categorizes these factors in three related groups: the aforementioned general factors that are being shared by the whole international donor community; inter-organizational factors influencing relationships which are especially important for UNDP in its coordinating role; and internal factors that UNDP can address to enhance its capacity. Taken together, these factors form some of the main building blocks for a strategy. The strategic issues constitute the most general level of discussion; the organizational issues are the most specific questions. All

TABLE 3
ISSUES AFFECTING UNDP'S ROLE IN PEACEBUILDING

1. UNDP Strategic Issues
General
In an environment originally characterized by a lack of preparedness, conceptual confusion on integrating relief, rehabilitation and development (continuum debate), declining resources and low confidence in the UN system,
- How to operationalize the SHD approach?
- How to integrate further relief, rehabilitation and development?
- How to further indiginize development cooperation and peacebuilding?
Specific Sub-questions
- What modes of execution are required and what does this imply for the tripartite system, in particular for the role of the government? Is the government in all cases the 'primary client?' *(And what are the implications for the concept of sovereignty?)*
- How do the types of conflict change and what are the implications for the functioning of UNDP/ERD?
- How to become more participatory with the local population in both general development cooperation and peacebuilding?

2. Inter-organizational Issues
General
In an environment where international donors do not provide enough money to let UNDP's central funding role materialize and where its coordinating role is often resisted,
- How can UNDP work better with other actors? Can it be more transparent?
Specific Sub-questions
- How are the modalities and practices of the UN Development Group worked out?
- When will UNDP's coordinating role take precedence; when will UNDP's own development cooperation activities come first? In other words, will the schizophrenia return?
- Will the Office of the United Nations Development Group be moved even closer to the Secretariat?
- What will be the relationship between UNDP and UNOPS with regard to execution? Will UNDP continue setting up its own executing office?
- How will the new relationships between DPA, OCHA and UNDP evolve particularly with regard to the integrated framework? What do these relationships imply for UNDP's coordinating role?
- How will the new division of roles between the Resident Coordinator/Res Rep and the humanitarian coordinator work?

3. Organizational Issues
General
- How to formulate a more integrated strategy for ERD's role in peacebuilding?
- Can UNDP build up sufficient in-house capacity? How does it expect to utilize its large field-presence, multi-sectoral outlook and neutral broker role without becoming too dispersed? How can it ensure that it is geared to field-level action and is able to deliver results?
- How can UNDP deal with the fundamental tension of being true to its original conception as a central, multi-sectoral and country-specific agency, while at the same time focusing itself more?
- When and how will the outcomes of UNDP's renewal process be evaluated, in particular with regard to decentralization? What will the follow-up be?
Specific Sub-questions
- What will be UNDP's priorities and/or comparative advantages in peacebuilding? How are they being realized?
- What is ERD's exact role in the Operations Support Unit?
- How will ERD cooperate with the now separately functioning Office of the United Nations Development Group?
- How will the relationship between ERD and the Regional Bureaux be worked out further?
- When and how will TRAC 3 money's impact be evaluated? What are the outcomes?
- Will ERD have a say in spending non-TRAC 3 money if there is no government?

of these questions may not form a complete strategy in the sense that this list of questions is not exhaustive, but they can complement the current reforms of both UNDP and the UN system.

Not all answers to the questions above will be unequivocal; there may be hard choices, difficult dilemmas and changes over time. But together they can contribute to a more outward-looking UNDP and thus help to strengthen UNDP's capacities.[55]

For the UN as a whole, the shortcomings of the current reform imply a need for a second Jackson report that studies the strategic issues for and capacities of the UN as a whole given its changing environment. The role of the governments in relation to local participation and modes of execution should be re-examined. It is not very likely, though still possible, that a new consensus resolution will ensue. For the time being, it is probably best to conclude that both UNDP reform and UN reform can be given the benefit of the doubt. They are necessary, but in all likelihood they have been too inward looking to be able to lead to more complete renewal.

Conclusions

Much of the criticism on UNDP in this article is not new. In 1994, the Administrator of UNDP himself presented an analysis to the Executive Board of UNDP, grouping criticism in three main areas:[56]

1. UNDP's weak substantive capacity.
2. Lack of clear mission and focus.
3. Its coordination role was not fully accepted by the UN system or fully realized by UNDP; and its central funding role not achieved.

It is difficult for UNDP to establish meaningful change in these areas because UNDP remains dependent on outside parties such as donor countries, recipient governments, local communities and UN organizations. In this respect UNDP is an intermediary organization balancing many different demands. Improving peacebuilding is even more difficult because UNDP is a newcomer in an environment initially characterized by a lack of preparedness, conceptual confusion on integrating relief, rehabilitation and development, decreasing resources and declining confidence in the UN system. In particular, many Western countries have no long-term development perspective on peacebuilding and they have not provided sufficient funding. This is not likely to change. Quite frequently in peacebuilding, country governments happily delegate the role of scapegoat to the UN system.

This article has shown the close linkages between development and peacebuilding, whereas the institutional make-up of the international system does not reflect this. The separation of peacekeeping from development has led to neglect of the role that UNDP, and development organizations in general, can play.

It has taken UNDP considerable time to respond to and become active in peacebuilding. At the same time, it had to attempt to strengthen its coordinating role. This required setting up ERD and creating as well as adapting policies, structures and procedures. Recently, UNDP as a whole initiated a large change process and the UN system also undertook reform.

All in all, UNDP has made steps in the right direction through SHD and UNDP 2001. These are necessary, but not sufficient conditions for success. UNDP needs to be more outward and forward looking to prevent the change process from becoming just another form of structural tinkering. UNDP cannot yet show that it has developed the capacity in peacebuilding that would let it gain more credibility both at the grassroots level and with the international community. Its great potential alone is not enough to be able to deliver results in peacebuilding.

ACKNOWLEDGEMENTS

The author would like to thank the many people in and outside UNDP who have helped with data-collection and checking this article.

NOTES

1. Steven Ratner, *The New UN Peacekeeping: Building Peace in Lands of Conflict After the Cold War*, London: Macmillan Press, 1995.
2. Kenneth Bush, 'Beyond Bungee Cord Humanitarianism: Towards a Developmental Agenda for Peacebuilding', *Canadian Journal of Development Studies*, Special Issue, 1996, pp.1–18.
3. War-torn Societies Project, *Rebuilding War-Torn Societies: An Action-Research Project on Problems of International Assistance in Post-Conflict Situations*, in mimeo, Geneva: UNRISD and PSIS, March 1995, 29 pp.
4. In this way, second generation peacekeeping is linked to the concept of positive peace which is a situation where conflicts are resolved non-violently and the possibility of war has been eradicated. See Johan Galtung, *Peace by Peaceful Means: Peace and Conflict, Development and* Civilizations, Oslo: PRIO and London: Sage Publications, 1996, pp.30–31.
5. For further discussion see Eva Bertram, 'Reinventing Governments: The Promise and Perils of United Nations Peacebuilding', *Journal of Conflict Resolution*, Vol.39, No.3, September 1995, pp.387–418, and Duane Bratt, 'Explaining Peacekeeping Performance: The UN in Internal Conflicts', *International Peacekeeping*, Vol.4, No.3, Autumn 1997, pp.45–70.
6. OECD/DAC has played a central role for donor countries in formulating and promoting guidelines for linking relief to development. For recent discussions, see also Claes Lindahl, 'Developmental Relief? An Issues Paper and an Annotated Bibliography on Linking Relief and Development', *SIDA Studies in Evaluation*, 96/3, Stockholm: SIDA Department for Evaluation and Internal Audit, 1996.
7. The difference between man-made and natural disasters is not always clear-cut. In the case of recurring natural disasters and/or a population that is already vulnerable, for example by moving into marginal lands or river basins due to overpopulation or environmental

degradation, the wider social and political system needs to be taken into account in order to understand the impact of and remedies to the disasters. See Mark Duffield, 'Complex Emergencies and the Crisis of Developmentalism', *IDS Bulletin*, Vol.25, No.4, 1994, pp.38–9, and Matthias Stiefel, *UNDP in Conflicts and Disasters: An Overview Report of the 'Continuum Project' (UNDP Project INT/93/79)*, in mimeo, Programme for Strategic and International Security Studies, Graduate Institute of International Studies, Geneva, August 1994 (revised edition), pp.15–17.

8. In addition, aid personnel were more frequently threatened and increasingly became victims of violence.

9. Bernard Wood, 'Lessons and Guidance for Donors: Key Points from the Development Assistance Committee's Guidelines on Conflict, Peace, and Development Cooperation', *USAID Conference: Promoting Democracy, Human Rights, and Reintegration in Post-Conflict Societies*, in mimeo, 30–31 October 1997, pp.15.

10. For examples, see Tim Allen (ed.) *In Search of Cool Ground: War, Flight & Homecoming in Northeast Africa*, Geneva: UNRISD in association with London: James Currey and Trenton: Africa World Press, 1996. The experience of the War-torn Societies Project also shows that donors should not overestimate their impact.

11. Jonathan Moore, *The UN and Complex Emergencies: Rehabilitation in Third World Transitions*, Geneva: UNRISD and War-torn Societies Project, 1996, pp.1–6.

12. Development and relief aid imply new availability and/or redistribution of resources. Since this can, *inter alia*, change the power balance in certain countries or regions, aid can also become a source of conflict. See for further analysis Mary Anderson, *Do No Harm: Supporting Local Capacities for Peace through Aid*, Cambridge: Collaborative for Development Action, Local Capacities for Peace Project, 1996.

13. Notice how the term 'continuum' combines related, yet analytically distinct concepts. On the one hand, it presumes a discrete continuation of the stages relief, rehabilitation, and development; on the other, it basically assumes that development is a linear sequence of which a disaster is only a temporary disruption.

14. Matthias Stiefel (see n.7), pp.16–17. Stiefel also provides further conceptual clarification, pp.15–22. See also Kenneth Bush (n.2), p.2.

15. Terence Ranger, *Concluding Reflections on Cross-Mandates*, in Tim Allen (ed.) *In Search of Cool Ground: War, Flight & Homecoming in Northeast Africa*, pp.322–4. Jolly argues that some successes in development cooperation are being underrated, in particular indicators of human development have improved considerably. See Richard Jolly, 'Human Development: The World After Copenhagen', *Global Governance*, Vol.3, No.2, May–Aug 1997, pp.233–48.

16. Duffield argues that crisis situations also reflect a crisis in developmentalism and its underlying modernist assumptions of continuing progress. In this sense, complex emergencies bring to light the dilemmas and problems that are less often noticed in regular development activities, but that are similar in many ways. See Mark Duffield, 'Complex Emergencies and the Crisis of Developmentalism', *IDS Bulletin*, Vol.25, No.4, 1994, pp.37–45.

17. Until recently, the amount of relief aid was growing considerably. This trend has now been reversed, which means that many relief organizations will have to scale down their operations.

18. The concept of nation building is also gaining currency, but its relationship with peacebuilding is insufficiently worked out.

19. Ministry of Foreign Affairs/DANIDA, *Strategies for Individual Organizations: Annex to the Plan of Action for Active Multilateralism*, 1996, Copenhagen, p.5.

20. See Dennis Dijkzeul, *The Management of Multilateral Organizations*, Boston: Kluwer Law International, 1997, p.29.

21. Douglas Williams, *The Specialized Agencies and the United Nations: The System in Crisis*, New York: St. Martin's Press, 1987, pp.18–25.

22. This office has been renamed three times. OPS is its third name.

23. It was rumour that DTCD, later named DDSMS, wished to acquire the staff posts of OPS. An earlier proposed merger between DTCD and OPS was cancelled in the end.

24. It will be interesting to see whether the Executive Board will allow this initiative or kill it as an unnecessary duplication and therefore a waste of resources. It may become a litmus test for finding out how serious national governments are about reforming the UN.
25. Ministry of Foreign Affairs/DANIDA, *Strategies for Individual Organizations* (see n.19), p.5.
26. UNDP Mission Statement.
27. Ministry of Foreign Affairs/DANIDA, *Strategies for Individual Organizations* (see n.19), p.6.
28. Ibid., pp.8–10.
29. ACC/1994/POQ/CRP.19/Annex, *Role and Functions of Resident Coordinators of the UN System's Operational Activities for Development: Arrangement for the Exercise of the Functions of the Resident Coordinator.*
30. Matthias Stiefel (see n.7), pp.23–4.
31. In this light it is unfortunate that some country governments still seem to push their own nationals for the Res Rep position. In such cases, political appointees do not necessarily possess the right qualities and it can demotivate other personnel. Generally, finding good staff for complex emergencies is difficult. Moore maintains that 'both the Secretariat and the operating agencies have to do a better job in filling key positions' in Jonathan Moore (see n.11), p.35. Matthias Stiefel (see n.7), pp.47–54, provides suggestions for reforming UNDP personnel policy and building up institutional expertise.
32. Res Rep's and country offices' initiatives have provided crucial contributions to peacebuilding in some countries. In Turkey, for example, the national SHD report's socio-economic analysis indicated in a diplomatic manner the need for specific policies concerning socio-economic needs in Southeast Turkey (Turkish Kurdistan). In Mali, the UNDP country office contributed to the resolution of the conflict in the North and the reconciliation and decentralization after the conflict.
33. UNDP, *Building Bridges Between Relief and Development: a Compendium of the UNDP Record in Crisis Countries*, Emergency Response Division, New York: UNDP, pp.2–3.
34. Matthias Stiefel (see n.7).
35. UNDP, *Building Bridges Between Relief and Development: a Compendium of the UNDP Record in Crisis Countries*, Emergency Response Division, New York: UNDP.
36. Michael Askwith, 'The Roles of DHA and UNDP in Linking Relief and Development', *IDS Bulletin*, Vol.25, No.4, 1994, pp.101–4.
37. Ibid. Resident Coordinators and Res Reps are also responsible for promoting the objectives of the International Decade for Natural Disaster Reduction. The IDNDR secretariat is part of the DHA office in Geneva.
38. UNDP, internal document, 6 March 1996.
39. Jonathan Moore (see n.11), p.50.
40. See James Gustave Speth, *Building a New UNDP: Agenda for Change* (Presentation by the Administrator to the UNDP Executive Board), New York: UNDP, 17 February 1994. For an overview of reform and change before 1996, see UNDP, *Change and Reform in UNDP: Highlights*, internal document, New York: UNDP, 1996.
41. UNDP, internal documents, 1996, 1997.
42. Ibid.
43. *UNDP News*, Special Edition on Change Management, July–August 1997, New York: UNDP, 1997 gives a simple, but good overview of UNDP's change process. See also James Gustave Speth, 'UNDP 2001 – Reform for Results', in *Development Today: Nordic Outlook on Development Assistance, Business and the Environment*, 23 July 1997, Oslo: Development Today A/S, p.11. For a more detailed overview: *UNDP 2001: Change Management Resource Guide*, Bureau of Planning and Resource Management, March 1998, New York: Bureau of Planning and Resource Management.
44. The SURFs are not supposed to become an additional organizational layer, which is a danger in many forms of decentralization and will need close scrutiny as implementation continues.
45. In the words of Hamel and Pralahad, UNDP is still not working on reinventing its 'industry' and regenerating its strategy. See Gary Hamel and C.K. Prahalad, *Competing for the Future*, Boston: Harvard Business School Press, 1994.

46. UNDP internal document: *UNDP 2001*, in mimeo, pp.6–7.
47. This lends support to Duffield's thesis that complex emergencies show a crisis of developmentalism.
48. The continuum debate can provide crucial insights on the interaction between the international community, UNDP, sub-national governments, NGOs and local communities.
49. See UNDP/ADM/97/58, *UNDP Headquarters: Main Features and Senior Managers*, in mimeo, New York: UNDP, 8 October 1997.
50. Such reforms increasingly look like a rite of passage for a new Secretary-General.
51. A/51/950, *Renewing the United Nations: A Programme for Reform, Report of the Secretary General*, New York: 14 July 1997. This report only offers cursory treatment of the institutional context at pp.12–13.
52. Joanna Macrae, 'Rearranging the Deck Chairs? Reforming the UN's Responses to Humanitarian Crises', *Relief and Rehabilitation Network Newsletter*, London: RRN, November 1997, pp.13–14.
53. It is not sufficiently clear whether DPA will only have political tasks, or whether it will also fulfil more operational tasks. The latter option can hamper UNDP.
54. See James Gustave Speth (n.43 above), pp.1–5. See also Andreas Zumach, 'Allzu zaghafte UNO-Reform', *E+Z*, 9 (1997), pp.237–9.
55. Richard Jolly, a political advisor to UNDP's Administrator, provides valuable advice on the operational characteristics of such a strategy (see n.15).
56. James Gustave Speth (see n.40), p.7.

The UN Specialized Agencies, Peacekeeping and the Enactment of Values

JIM WHITMAN

The values at the heart of the United Nations system and the major specialized agencies are diminished by the operational demands of humanitarian disasters and the necessity of working in tandem with peacekeeping operations. Emergency humanitarianism not only diverts human and material resources away from developmental expressions of humanitarian obligation, but also from the important normative work of the specialized agencies. It is argued that the greatest challenge facing the UN is how to restore the essentially developmental ethos of the organization – and the specialized agencies in particular – in the face of humanitarian emergencies of the number and severity now extant.

In the same way that many perceive the role of the United Nations as all but synonymous with peacekeeping activities, it is not difficult to regard the work of its specialized agencies[1] as largely comprising operations within or beside peacekeeping missions and related, humanitarian emergencies. The scholarship devoted to their performance as operational bodies in Bosnia, Somalia, Rwanda and elsewhere is greatly in excess of more general considerations of their organization and purposes, and of the loose system they comprise.[2] This might seem unsurprising – and indeed, appropriate – given their strenuous efforts to deal with the consequences of war, genocide, forced displacement and hunger. The gravity and extent of the human suffering involved in the fieldwork imparts a moral character to analyses of success and failure as well as deliberations over reform. The question naturally arises, how can we improve the effectiveness of our institutional responses to disasters of this character and scale – how, we might ask, to give appropriate expression to our humanitarian ideals?

Yet even while UN and agency-specific reforms continue apace – many dedicated to improving the efficiency of humanitarian response – the UN-mandated sanctions against Iraq are causing suffering which is an affront to humane decency. And much the most reliable detail of the grim realities there comes from the agencies themselves: FAO, UNICEF, WFP and WHO.

Jim Whitman is a member of the Faculty of Social and Political Sciences at Cambridge University.

A recent survey conducted by UNICEF in conjunction with WFP and the Iraqi government found that nearly one million children under the age of five are chronically malnourished.[3] A second oil-for-food agreement approved by the Security Council in February 1998 appears as unlikely to make a swift and substantial difference as the first,[4] and there seems little prospect that the sanctions will be lifted in the near future. It has been estimated that as many as one million Iraqis have died since the imposition of the sanctions in 1990.

One may agonize over the supposed correlation between the logistical efficiency and political efficacy of sanctions, particularly in this case; meanwhile, UNICEF and its sister organizations struggle to mitigate its human consequences. They do so with grossly inadequate means in steadily deteriorating circumstances and in the face of the mandate of the United Nations of which they are a part. There is nothing in contemporary international affairs which so starkly illustrates the tension in the UN system between the enforcement of order and the enactment of values; between Chapter VII of the UN Charter and the reaffirmation of 'faith in fundamental human rights [and] the dignity and worth of the human person' of its preamble. Little in the recent history of peacekeeping[5] encourages us to face this – after all, it is frequently military force which opens up the 'humanitarian space' for a range of UN and other actors to conduct emergency relief. However, what makes the position of the specialized agencies so invidious in this case is that those present in Iraq are upholding values as much as saving lives and relieving hardship – not against the brutalizing effects of war and societal breakdown, but as a result of the United Nations acting to 'maintain international peace and stability'.

The uniqueness of the case should not obscure the fact that it arises from the wider and more visible political reality in which bilateral and inter-governmental (including UN) humanitarianism is conceived, organized and managed.[6] Here we have not simple oversight, not the 'invisible starving' or what is loosely characterized as a 'lack of political will' – indeed, quite the reverse is the case. But is the antithesis of the dysfunction being played out in Iraq to be found in the concerted effort entailed in peacekeeping operations and the simultaneous or subsequent humanitarian work of the specialized agencies and others? The subject of this essay is the manner and degree to which the humanitarian ideals of the main specialized agencies of the UN find expression; the extent to which peacekeeping activities detract from this potential; and the agencies' capacity for giving strength and voice – and not merely a remission of suffering – to 'we the peoples'.

The Specialized Agencies and Humanitarian Ideals

One of the least benign outcomes of peacekeeping in this decade is that the term 'humanitarianism' should now more readily be associated with emergency provision than with development. Yet at the foundation of the United Nations enterprise – in the Preamble and Article 55 of the Charter; in the Universal Declaration of Human Rights; and in the constitutions of the specialized agencies – one finds an acknowledgement of and commitment to core human values. Of course, even 'economic and social advancement' was never uncontentious and the United Nations is a political organization, not a humanitarian one. Despite an organizational arrangement, 'the main goal [of which] was to avoid politicization of…economic and social cooperation and focus instead on the technical aspects, so as not to endanger effective and universal activities',[7] the hope that political matters could be confined to the General Assembly and the Security Council was never likely to prove successful. The larger conflicts and tensions in the international political arena – not least the impacts of decolonization, and the differences between the West, the Soviet bloc and the Non-Aligned Movement – also found ready expression in the specialized agencies and their relationships with member states.[8]

While all states are practised at maximizing advantage within the bounds of what the UN system will allow, Article 57 of the Charter ensures that for all of them, the terms by which the specialized agencies are brought into relationship with the United Nations can be set as functional as opposed to political. The integrity of the UN system, at least as conceived by its member states, is thereby preserved and the agencies undertake essentially collaborative work, furthering cooperation between states by familiar means, including 'recommend[ing] such international agreements as may be necessary'.[9] However, even what were once the most straight-forwardly technical matters, such as regularizing international communications, become fraught with political difficulties as the postal system is supplanted by telecommunications and the 'free exchange of ideas and knowledge' meets intellectual property rights. States will defend their interests in any field of activity against perceived intrusion by a specialized agency, most readily with the charge of 'politicization'.[10]

These sensitivities grow in proportion as the work of the specialized agencies engages individuals and communities in ways which conflict with, or are perceived to threaten, the interests of states. The agencies are established by intergovernmental agreement and were created to 'observe, coordinate, and recommend measures, and to propose rules to their member states that should be laid down in international treaties between the states',[11] which would suggest that the preambular language of their constitutions is largely declaratory and that their room for manoeuvre beyond facilitating international cooperation is quite constrained. However, the cumulative effect of their 50 years of technical, developmental, educational, scientific, cultural and protective endeavours has moral weight and political meaning as well as practical outcomes. For all that the human values driving this work are often implicit, they are nevertheless discernible and, over time, prominent. In the same way that human rights take root in the world as much through individual and community recognition of entitlement as through the enforcement of international legal instruments, the specialized agencies have given expression and emphasis to the *fact* of human worth; to human rights which are *a priori* the obligations of citizenship; and to the claims of adults and children alike to minimum physical and political standards of living.

These values, usually expressed as humanitarian ideals, are evinced in the work of the specialized agencies in three ways. The first is through direct enunciation, constitutionally and through their numerous publications,[12] and given force and momentum by extending to most of humanity and touching on everything from the rights of displaced peoples to the Universal Declaration on the Human Genome and Human Rights.[13]

The second is through enactment in accordance with their intergovernmental remits. This takes the form of initiating the discussions on an impressive range of international and increasingly global issues, and of forwarding international law, declarations, standards and basic principles. The World Food Summit, the UN Conferences on the environment, women, children, human rights and human settlements (Habitat II) are impressive not only in scale but also in the fact that they cannot but engage human values as well as matters technical and legal. The now standard presence of parallel NGO forums at these conferences further highlights issues of political and diplomatic sensitivity. That the goal of eliminating hunger has given way to an international determination to reduce it is not a defeat for the FAO; together with the other specialized agencies, their work to deal with the consequent human suffering serves as a rebuke to the diminution of states' resolve. And the wider communities that they engaged through the organization of the World Food Summit are better connected to one another and better poised to continue their technical, educational and lobbying efforts.

Contention over basic human values is not always a matter of recalcitrant states holding out against a universalizing norm. For example, as many have observed, 'Throughout the history of the human rights regime, less developed states have resisted [a] limited conception of rights and attempted to promote rights that supported their demand for economic security and development.'[14] Likewise, there runs the argument that 'local custom should prevail over royal decree' – in this case, that human rights are culturally mediated, a subject particularly sensitive with respect to gender issues, but also extending to more general conceptions of human rights.[15] Yet contention is as much to be welcomed as expected. The struggle to achieve, maintain and further human rights within and between states is not movement towards a fixed goal, determined in the West or anywhere else; rather, the work *arises* from shared values – in a recognition of the worth and dignity of the human person, clearly enshrined in the ethos of each of the specialized agencies.[16] Whether or not one subscribes to the view that the advancement of human rights is to some degree a 'hegemonic imposition', and however one might conceive 'sustainable economic prosperity', it is plain that in a world beset with 800 million malnourished human beings and a widening gap between rich and poor, that serious engagement with values is an essential prerequisite to programmatic efficiency.

In a counterpart to the tension between 'international peace and security' on the one hand and the betterment of conditions for individuals and communities on the other, the values given expression by the specialized agencies stand in contrast to the systemic concerns and strictures of the Bretton Woods institutions, particularly the IMF. Here again, the work of the agencies in impoverished regions has often run against the grain of the larger preoccupation with economic stability and powerful states' interests in maintaining the essential features of the world political economy. Between 1990 and 1993, for example, Zambia spent 35 times as much on debt repayments as it did on education. Similar statistics on the willful, albeit indirect impoverishment of nations and peoples – in health, housing, nutrition and the other fundaments of human welfare – are abundant. Directly, in operational terms, the specialized agencies can do little more than alleviate the worst in such circumstances, but the principled and effectively oppositional character of their work – and that of others, including NGOs – provides much of the moral force and often, much of the detailed information which generates and sustains movement for change.

It would be misleading to characterize the humanitarian ideals of the specialized agencies and the perceived interests of states (both direct and as expressed through the United Nations) as being all but entirely oppositional. In fact, the standing and political disinterestedness of the agencies allows them to create arenas for deliberation and action on a range of difficult and sometimes sensitive issues, such as climate change and the HIV/AIDS epidemic.[17] This traffic moves in both directions. For example, behind the credit which accrued to WHO for the eradication of smallpox was an astute and benign calculation of immediate and long-term benefits:

> The CDC [the Centers for Disease Control, Atlanta] made a decision to put 300 people into smallpox eradication. Smallpox was eradicated because the leadership of the CDC made the decision that it would keep a low profile and allow WHO to have the credit for this in the hope that it would strengthen WHO for other things.[18]

When measured against the nature and scale of human need, the specialized agencies' enactment of human values might seem pitifully small, yet their capacity to bring about normative change, though often indirect and diffuse, is nevertheless powerful in respect of their potential to energize, educate and empower and – perhaps most importantly – to create expectations. R.B.J. Walker's assertion about critical social movements is no less true of the specialized agencies: that they '...are important not because they have the immediate capacity to induce existing elites to pursue more enlightened policies but because they participate in a more far-reaching reinvention of political life'.[19]

The third way in which the specialized agencies give expression to humanitarian ideals is in defending or re-establishing them as part of, or in conjunction with, the international community's response to certain violent or potentially violent conflicts – peacekeeping. Those who regard the development and extension of peacekeeping since 1989 as a largely positive if limited phenomenon might incline towards the view of the poet Robinson Jeffers: 'Old violence is not too old to beget new values.' However, the values that are grossly and routinely violated in war, state collapse and politically-driven violence could not be more basic. That we have not found it within our capacities to respond at all to some instances of genocide should tell us as much about the enactment of our professed values as about our willingness to enforce international law. Peacekeeping missions with a predominant or considerable emergency relief element represent a double failure: the larger United Nations remit – to maintain international peace and security – is breached; and the human values inherent in the orientation of the UN and its agencies alike suffer a setback. The damage done to the normative tenor of international life by the re-emergence of genocide is incalculable and will continue to haunt our efforts to establish humane governance;[20] and it is likely that the number and severity of other violent humanitarian disasters – not all of which meet with a response – is cumulatively little less pernicious. The main UN agencies which now deal with the individual and social consequences of war and its aftermath undertake these formidable tasks with a moral and professional urgency frequently at odds with funding and support arrangements which impart an ad hoc quality and unhelpful constraints on their activities.[21] The sense in which these inadequacies add insult to injury is profound.

For international actors, the notion of 'pure' humanitarianism does not arise, but since political purposes are driven by perceived interests and informed by values, our omissions articulate these as clearly as our actions. Short of stabilizing preventive deployments and/or development initiatives which strengthen social coherence, peacekeeping operations and their attendant humanitarian initiatives can be said to represent a defence of humanitarian ideals only in a qualified sense – a point clearly lost in media representations of the innocent suffering and virtuous or heroic relief efforts. It could well be said that emergency responses, particularly those which require some degree of military presence or participation, do at least ensure that the ideal of a world order founded on basic human values is not abandoned altogether. But what is lost from view – and driven ever further from active consideration – is a serious examination of the purposes and beneficiaries of humanitarianism. There are several reasons for this: a conception of humanitarian need largely confined to large-scale, visible suffering; the presence of national militaries on time-limited deployments and with public expectation divided between a concern for casualties and measures of 'success'; inadequate resources for uncertain durations; and – perhaps worst of all – a familiarity with politically-driven humanitarian disasters such as to make them appear routine. Humanitarian obligation becomes 'compassion fatigue'. And at the international level, this takes the form of 'normalizing emergencies'[22] and a gradual accommodation with the grossly iniquitous and unstable world order of which they are a part, against which the specialized agencies – like peacekeeping forces – can sometimes practice little more than containment.

The Specialized Agencies and Peacekeeping

The establishment of peacekeeping was a creative response to a Cold War crisis and Security Council deadlock. On a small scale and a consensual basis, the lack of operational, administrative and coordinating mechanisms within the UN secretariat did occasionally cause the organization and the Secretary-General[23] some difficulties, but none were crises in the scale of things. The post-Cold War extension of peacekeeping – interventionist, large-scale and with considerable, often pressing humanitarian claims – was a change of kind as well as degree. Among the adaptations required was a re-ordering of the priorities of the specialized agencies, their relationship to these operations, and the establishment of working relationships between the agencies, national militaries and NGOs, often at short notice and in the most stressful of circumstances.[24]

What is of particular note in these adjustments has been the reorientation of the specialized agencies away from development to emergency relief –

which now accounts for 66 per cent of operational expenditures by the World Food Programme, for example.[25] This has combined powerfully with a sharp reduction in development assistance which has fallen by 17 per cent since 1992, while the total development assistance of OECD/EU countries as gauged by the Development Assistance Committee is now at its lowest point since records began in 1950.[26] One need not advance an argument about causal relations between under-development and current levels of emergency provision, nor attempt a statistical disaggregation of provision for 'natural' disasters from that for the outcomes of political violence, in order to discern that the trend is moving rapidly towards a hardening relationship between the rich and poor worlds. Behind a popular perception of charitable and occasionally risk-taking beneficence is the reality of political disengagement and a humanitarianism which, for all its poignant qualities, is shifting from the betterment of life to saving lives in some instances – often as the complement to or objective of peacekeeping activities.

This works to the detriment of the specialized agencies and the larger United Nations since 'maintaining peace and security' is impoverished to the same extent as 'humanitarian obligation': government calculations of risk and commitment rarely exceed the bounds of their more familiar interests;[27] deeply impacted human turmoil and suffering is framed in terms of emergencies amenable to the available, typically time-limited means; and the enforcement of order and relief components of these enterprises reinforces the notion that these are the restorative counterparts to an interrupted 'peace' and 'development'.[28] The least edifying instance of this formulation was the belatedly-sanctioned French Operation *Turquoise* in Rwanda. As the contingent in Goma undertook the digging of mass graves, the French Defence Minister was moved to write, 'We have stopped the violence, cared for the victims and prepared the way for those who deserve the beautiful name of humanitarians'.[29] Four years later, the work of the humanitarians, though less immediately acute, is every bit as daunting; meanwhile, it is reliably reported that the French government is seeking to restore its influence in the region through the incitement of rebel forces in the Democratic Republic of Congo.[30]

Perhaps worst of all, as humanitarianism comes to be ever more closely associated with large-scale emergencies and interventionist peacekeeping, the compass of the work shrinks – ironically, with further burdens being placed upon the specialized agencies. When politico-military and humanitarian missions share the same field of operations – whether or not they are formally aligned – the work of the specialized agencies and other humanitarian actors is greatly complicated and sometimes compromised. The struggle to reconcile moral principles, operational tenets[31] and practical

requirements underpins even development work, but in militarized
humanitarian emergencies, these are approached through (and difficult to
separate from) the requirements and constraints of peacekeeping.

Political Tasks, Humanitarian Responsibilities

Although not the first instance of military-humanitarian cooperation, the
Chapter VII resolutions authorizing interventions by both UNITAF and
UNOSOM II were the first to be undertaken for the specific purpose of
ensuring the delivery of humanitarian aid. What has sometimes been
characterized as the militarization of humanitarian assistance[32] was
confirmed in that arena when a number of NGOs and even the ICRC hired
armed escorts for the delivery of their aid – and this practice has spread.

In the same way that impartiality in peacekeeping is as much a matter of
perception as professed intent, the notion that humanitarian assistance could
be delivered without political meaning or impact might be a comforting
illusion for some humanitarians, but even bilateral relief for natural
disasters is politically shaped and directed. When the specialized agencies
(and NGOs) work in conjunction with intervening soldiers, the arena is
politically charged as well as operationally challenging in more familiar
ways. The anxiety of states to confine the UN agencies to functional roles,
assisting rather than transgressing sovereign prerogatives and priorities,
does not arise in the case of truly volatile or impacted peacekeeping
missions. In these cases, the assumption of a range of political
responsibilities – as was the case in Bosnia with the UNHCR's lead agency
status and incorporation of the internally displaced within its competence –
furthers national and inter-governmental purposes, if only in respect of their
not becoming 'entangled'.[33]

In Bosnia, UNHCR was many times faced with the dilemma of knowing
that its best chance of protecting beleaguered minority populations –
helping to evacuate them to safer areas – was effectively cooperating with
'ethnic cleansing'. And after the Dayton Peace Accord, which contains
specific provision for the return of exiled and displaced populations to their
home regions for the elections, UNHCR found itself without adequate
enforcement from IFOR to ensure minority repatriation. The High
Commissioner for Refugees, Sadako Ogata, felt herself obliged to
emphasize the principle against the impossibility of enacting it: 'The
priority will have to be on returns to majority areas. This is what is most doable and safest given the conditions on the ground. But let me be very clear:
we should continue to insist on the right of everyone to return to their homes
wherever these may be – including minority areas.'[34]

The fusion of political tasks and humanitarian responsibilities in an
instance of this kind is unlikely to occur in a situation other than one in

which it is important that something is seen to be done (or attempted), and unfortunately the agency is most likely to be perceived as having failed in its core humanitarian remit, as well as bringing its more general competence into question. Notwithstanding the unique intensities of the Bosnian conflict and the special position of the UNHCR within it, difficult, politically sensitive problems are familiar to all agencies working in militarily contested lands and on behalf of the threatened, vulnerable and displaced. However accurate it might be to say that humanitarian assistance has now become militarized,[35] it has certainly become politicized: in addition to the perceptions of antagonists and aid recipients alike, all parties find an expanded field in which to act, and it is the humanitarians who find themselves with what Cedric Thornberry has described as a classic dilemma:

> What are international peace and humanitarian personnel to do in the absence of the parties' consent, or in an environment of qualified consent? UNHCR and ICRC have at various times indicated that force is not the answer; one cannot achieve humanitarian goals by fighting one's way through. If withdrawal, also, is not an alternative, how does one function on the dangerous, shifting sands in the middle?[36]

Blockades, efforts to lever political ends from humanitarian imperatives (and vice-versa), manipulation of the international media, and intransigent demands for 'reciprocity' have all found their place in 'complex peacekeeping'. The politicization of humanitarian assistance can also extend beyond the immediate span of a peacekeeping mission:

> The Kigali government is frustrated by the failure – as it sees it – of the international community to offer aid or fulfil its promises of support, and furious at donor talk of aid 'conditionality' about human rights, for example, when no such conditions were considered for refugees whose ranks include mass murderers. Suspicious that agencies are exploiting the 'emergency' to maintain their income, Rwanda has resorted to taxing donor-backed aid agencies for vehicles, radio and imported supplies, normally exempt from duties, in an attempt to get some money from governments.[37]

The representatives of specialized agencies in militarized though less fraught circumstances often feel the necessity of distancing themselves from the political objectives of the peacekeeping mission – or popular perceptions of these. In other words, within the 'humanitarian space' created by the military for the humanitarians, the latter must sometimes establish yet another.[38] To this must be added that the political goals of a peacekeeping mission can be inconsistent or even contradictory (as was the case with UNPROFOR), and that the governments of national military contingents have exercised considerable independence in interpreting Security Council mandates (UNITAF and UNOSOM II).

Goals and Commitment

One of the difficulties for specialized agency and other humanitarian effort which comes to share the field with a peacekeeping operation is that owing to the public and political meanings of the dispatch of troops for humanitarian purposes (in however broad a sense of that term), the *fact* of commitment all too easily displaces concern for its quality and duration. Humanitarian need clearly extends well beyond the formal end of peacekeeping missions (and most often, long before they start) and once political and media attention has peaked, important, sometimes crucial matters, such as demining and demobilization, are left not only as further operational tasks or obstacles, but also as competing claims on scarce and diminishing resources. The formidable difficulties with which humanitarian actors in Angola have had to grapple – before, during and after the three UN peacekeeping missions (themselves grossly under-resourced) – continue with specialized agency emergency appeals for that country, the latest of which (April, 1998) received only 11 per cent of the required funds.

In an era of accountability to donors, any recipient operational body will want to demonstrate clearly articulated and verifiable goals, but in combination with short-term and appeal-based funding, the extent to which they are able to make long-term commitments and establish coherent plans is severely constrained. And in emergency situations, humanitarian ideals are brought into their most narrow focus: dealing with cholera outbreaks instead of immunization programmes; clean water and sanitation in refugee camps instead of in villages and towns; emergency feeding before agricultural development.

Not every increase in operational activity (emergency or otherwise) will entail a loss for the more normative work of the specialized agencies. UNICEF has long excelled at programmes by which it plausibly claims to have saved the lives of 20 million children, and it has ambitious plans to further its work in areas ranging from the provision of safe water and sanitation to family planning.[39] And behind these accomplishments is its achievement of the Convention on the Rights of the Child – the most widely endorsed human rights treaty; moreover, UNICEF is energetically pursuing its implementation. As one analyst has observed, 'That the organization has been allowed by member states to take upon itself the task of implementing a human rights agreement, and that it has the ability to actually work within states and to take the initiative, is significant and suggests a new model for future human rights instruments'.[40] Yet what appears to be a balance in its range of activities is in fact a juggling act, since, like UNDP and UNHCR, the sense in which UNICEF is a 'specialized agency' is operational, not constitutional and all three must therefore rely for funding on voluntary donations and not through assessed contributions. This means that unanticipated natural or politically-driven disasters can severely impact upon short and medium-term commitments which even in the normal course of things are subject to the vagaries of international 'recognition' and states' preferences. Peacekeeping missions, whether or not they are generally perceived to have been successful, can easily exhaust public interest already saturated with images of human suffering of the worst and most dramatic kind. What price post-conflict peacebuilding and a 'relief-to-development continuum'?[41]

Coordination

The coordination of humanitarian assistance, a phrase most commonly employed with respect to the military–civil–UN relationships in 'complex emergencies' also has meaning within the humanitarian communities and specifically, between the specialized agencies. There is considerable overlap in the fundaments of any field operation, most notably logistics, and when the need is most pressing, the agencies have shown an admirable degree of flexibility, sharing limited resources and undertaking specific tasks, jointly or on others' behalf (sometimes including NGOs). This has also extended to the timely transmission of information, including WFP's weekly situation reports, UNHCR's humanitarian updates from the Great Lakes region and the various Integrated Regional Information Networks.

However, the operational autonomy of the specialized agencies, together with stressed, under-financed and resourced field presences, exposes what passes for coordination between them as more an expression of cooperative burden-sharing than managerial imperatives, the recent adoption of 'lead agencies' notwithstanding. The following example from the Great Lakes region in 1997 illustrates this:

> UNICEF has renounced its role as lead agency in the non-food sector in light of its leadership commitments in other sectors (e.g. water/sanitation) and its limited capacity in the non-food sector. However, UNICEF will continue to participate in the planning and implementation of activities in the non-food sector under the coordination of another organisation. Discussions are underway as to who will now do this job.[42]

In any event, field coordination, no less than setting achievable goals, is conditioned by the political commitment of the world's more powerful states. For all that peacekeeping operations can be impressive, militarily and politically, many can fairly be characterized as belated and palliative, and the extent to which the work of the specialized agencies benefit directly from peacekeeping operations is all too brief. In international political terms, the job is finished quickly; in humanitarian terms, the work persists. Even forward-looking efforts to order an international response to common but difficult and geographically dispersed humanitarian issues is frustrated by the lack of genuine and sustained willingness on the part of those states with the power to back them. Consider the plight of displaced persons, whose daily care absorbs a good deal of the attention of the specialized agencies in the field:

> The Secretary-General's representative on internally displaced persons, Francis Deng, after reviewing the situation in Burundi, El Salvador, the Russian Federation, Rwanda, Somalia, Sri Lanka, Sudan and the former Yugoslavia, concluded that consultations with the 'pertinent circles in the international community' had convinced him that 'the available options for improving protection of and assistance to internally displaced persons are clearly limited'. In fact, he saw his own mandate as 'an excuse for inaction by the international community'.[43]

Funding

The Special Representative of the Secretary-General (SRSG) for the peacekeeping mission for Angola (UNAVEM II), Margaret Anstee, characterized the funding arrangements for the mission as a 'pattern of utmost parsimony'. She recounts:

> Not only was the Security Council a non-starter as a source of additional resources, but procedures for obtaining money through formal UN channels were too cumbersome... I concluded that the only way out was to seek timely contributions *in kind* from donors, in the form of transport (including the loan of hire aircraft), services (for example, printing) and supplies (for example, paper), as well as perhaps personnel. I suggested to [Marrack Goulding] that such an approach might even have wider relevance, given the international community's desire to have bigger and better UN peacekeeping operations at cut-price rates, on the one hand, and the UN's limited operational capacity on the other.[44]

This instance is not representative, certainly compared with expenditures in Cambodia and the former Yugoslavia, but it is indicative of the extent to which the resolve of Security Council resolutions can mask the paucity of means extended by states to enact them. And the 'pattern of parsimony' extends to the specialized agencies, through assessed budgets unable to stretch, voluntary contributions which do not materialize or remits which depend upon special emergency appeals.[45]

In addition, the UN funds and programmes subject to voluntary funding are to some extent in competition with NGOs. As one study reports, 'Even the ICRC, one of the most financially stable of humanitarian organizations, has experienced cash flow problems in recent years. Other organizations which have had annual expenditures exceeding annual income in recent years include UNHCR, Oxfam, Save the Children, the International Organisation for Migration and Concern'.[46] The humanitarian crises which engender peacekeeping operations in some instances are not greatly diminished thereby, but the resources available to the full range of humanitarian actors are. (The UN funds and programmes rely on only ten countries for as much as 90 per cent of their funds.) All of this further impacts on the ability of the concerned bodies to coordinate or cooperate at a managerial level instead of in the field by force of circumstances.

Making the System Work vs the Work of the System

The emergence and persistence of so many humanitarian emergencies – of which only a fraction are met with peacekeeping initiatives – militate against a thorough re-consideration of the purpose, priorities and structure of the specialized agencies. In the emergency ethos in which they now operate, any consideration of humanitarian obligation is supplanted by the demands of 'fire-fighting'; management is eschewed for managerialism; renewal gives way to 'reform'. Perhaps the centre of gravity in this is not the UN reform process of 1997, but the 50th anniversary observances two years earlier. Much of the anti-visionary tone, the 'doing more with less' mentality of official as well as state pronouncements and the failure to recognize and promote the essential, normative features of the UN system found institutional expression two years later. Hannah Arendt might have been addressing the UN reform process – in prospect or after the fact – when she wrote, 'It has always been a great temptation, for men of action no less than men of thought, to find a substitute for action in the hope that the realm of human affairs may escape the haphazardness and moral irresponsibility inherent in a plurality of actors.'[47]

For many of those concerned with the humanitarian aspects of peacekeeping, the central concern is how to make the system work, succinctly expressed by Antonio Donini: 'Should the humanitarians be better equipped by the international community to do their job or should the military be trained to take on tasks other than war and security?'[48] This is neatly characterized but difficult to address, not least because it is as much a political as a conceptual question. More difficult still is a re-consideration of the work of the system, the context in which these and related operational dilemmas are played out: how can the United Nations begin to make the transition away from an emergency orientation back towards its developmental ethos?

In view of the extent and character of humanitarian need, this might appear a highly impractical concern, not least for humanitarian operatives who cannot but respond to life-threatening situations, however much that might detract from carefully-laid plans. Yet the pertinence of this concern can perhaps best be seen by inverting the question: 'To what extent does emergency humanitarianism detract from the enactment of values as enshrined in the United Nations system?' and instead ask, 'What values have been evinced in this decade of intense emergency humanitarianism?'

Stepping back from the question of whether the United Nations system has the capacity for effective disaster management, it is worth asking whether the entrenched poverty, structural inequalities and debilitated social infrastructures which sometimes precede and nearly always follow humanitarian disasters can be alleviated on a scale worthy of our professed ideals in the current climate. Perhaps we are creating our own complex dependencies. The literature on development has a long history of dependency theory, but consider how the specialized agencies themselves are dependent on a small number of donor governments; that a sizeable portion of their staffs, capacities, response mechanisms and most successful appeals for voluntary contributions arises from well-publicized emergencies; and that careerism and the defence of 'turf' militate against what should lay at the heart of any proper developmental ethos – 'to make ourselves redundant'. As objectives become donor driven, particularly as we enter a period of shrinking funds and increased competition, the self-protective nature of organizations and bureaucracies can be expected to come into full play. There is a sense, therefore, in which the professionalization of emergency assistance helps to entrench it – in terms of public acceptance as well as institutional fixtures. There is also the question of accountability. Donors and agencies, both UN and private, are closely bound to one another, their politics essentially complementary. Like the difference between the enactment of a law and its enforcement, humanitarianism undertaken in conjunction with peacekeeping diminishes rather than strengthens the ethos. Put more starkly, could it be said that emergency humanitarianism supports the very status quo which engenders it?

The former Executive Director of the World Food Programme, James Ingram, has argued that 'the time has come for the United Nations to vacate the humanitarian relief field' and has posed an internationalized ICRC as an alternative model.[49] Whatever the political and operational possibilities of this idea or its variants, its attraction is not merely as an alternative that might be more effective operationally, but also as one which might restore the specialized agencies to their remits. It is difficult to conceive of any plausible organizational form within the current international system which could quickly dispel the familiar inadequacies, tensions and dilemmas of humanitarian field work, but much the most important conceptual work before us is to consider how to answer the anguish of human suffering while simultaneously working on the diminution of its causes.

NOTES

1. The term 'specialized agency' is used throughout in an operational sense. In legal and UN institutional terms, the major specialized agencies include the World Health Organization, the Food and Agriculture Organization and UNESCO; the major Programmes and Funds include UNICEF, the World Food Programme, the United Nations Development Programme and the United Nations High Commission for Refugees.
2. See Douglas Williams, *The Specialized Agencies and the United Nations: The System in Crisis*, New York: St Martin's Press, 1987; for a detailed study of a single UN specialized agency see Javed Siddiqi, *World Health and World Politics: The World Health Organization and the U.N. System*, London: Hurst and Company, 1995.
3. UNICEF Information Newsline, 'Nearly One Million Children Malnourished in Iraq, says UNICEF', http://www.unicef.org/newsline/97pr60.htm
4. A WFP report points out, 'The plan is contingent on Iraq selling some $4.5 billion worth of oil over the next six months, with roughly three billion dollars earmarked for humanitarian supplies and emergency infrastructure repairs. A team of UN oil experts, however, has concluded that $300 million is required for rehabilitation of the oil sector as Iraq is going to begin approaching the pumping capacity to meet the six-month target'. Report No.23, 5 June 1998,
5. 'Peacekeeping' is used throughout in its widest sense, including what is now commonly referred to as 'classic' peacekeeping (as in UNFICYP) as well as mandates under the Chapter VII enforcement powers of the Security Council (as in Somalia.)
6. Although its emphasis is on development cooperation, a useful and indicative survey is EUROSTEP/ICVA, *The Reality of Aid 1997–1998: An Independent Review of Development Cooperation*, London: Earthscan, 1997.
7. Bruno Simma (ed.), *The Charter of the United Nations: A Commentary*, Oxford: Oxford University Press, 1994, p.804.
8. See for example, Mark F. Imber, *The USA, ILO, UNESCO and IAEA: Politicization and Withdrawal in the Specialized Agencies*, London: Macmillan, 1989.
9. UNESCO constitution.
10. For a useful if now somewhat dated study, see Clare Wells, *The UN, UNESCO and the Politics of Knowledge*, London: Macmillan, 1987.
11. Simma (see N.7), p.800.
12. Perhaps most evident in UNESCO, *Birthright of Man* (A selection of texts prepared under the direction of Jeanne Hersch), Paris: UNESCO, 1969.
13. http://www.unesco.org/ibc/uk/genome/projet/index.html
14. Tony Evans, 'Universal Human Rights: Imposing Values', in Caroline Thomas and Peter Wilkins, *Globalization and the South*, London: Macmillan, 1997, p.92.
15. See David R. Penna and Patricia J. Campbell, 'Human Rights and Culture: Beyond Universality and Relativism, *Third World Quarterly*, Vol.19, No.1, pp.7–27.
16. This is not to say that human rights have not been used as a political or diplomatic lever, or that the idea cannot be attached to or incorporated in larger political and economic agendas.
17. See, for example, A.J. McMichael, A. Haines, R. Slooff and S. Kovats (eds), *Climate Change*

and Human Health (An assessment prepared by a task Group on behalf of the World Health Organization, The World Meteorological Organization and the United Nations Environment Programme), Geneva: WHO, 1996; UNAIDS (UNICEF, UNDP, UNFPA, UNESCO, WHO, World Bank) and WHO, *Report on the Global HIV/AIDS Epidemic*, June 1998.

18. William Foege, 'Surveillance, Eradication and Control: Successes and Failures', in Jim Whitman (ed.), *The Politics of Emerging and Resurgent Infectious Diseases*, Macmillan, forthcoming.

19. R.B.J. Walker, *One World, Many Worlds: Struggles for a Just World Peace*, Boulder: Lynne Rienner Publishers, 1988, p.8

20. See Richard Falk, *On Humane Governance: Toward a New Global Politics* Cambridge: Polity Press, 1995.

21. For indicative agency overviews, see UNICEF, *The State of the World's Children 1996*, Oxford: Oxford University Press for UNICEF; UNHCR, *The State of the World's Refugees: A Humanitarian Agenda*, Oxford: Oxford University Press for UNHCR, 1997.

22. Mark Bradbury, 'Normalising the Crisis in Africa', *Journal of Humanitarian Assistance*, , posted 19 March 1998.

23. See Trygve Lie, *In the Cause of Peace*, New York: Macmillan, 1954, particularly Chapter XVIII on Korea.

24. Jim Whitman and David Pocock (eds), *After Rwanda: the Coordination of United Nations Humanitarian Assistance*, London: Macmillan, 1996.

25. http://www.wfp.org./reports/wfpstats/97/tab1-97.html It is also noteworthy that in 1990, 65 per cent of UNICEF's funds were available for general purposes and regular programmes, but by 1995, this had fallen to 53 per cent.

26. EUROSTEP/ICVA, *The Reality of Aid 1997–1998* (see N.6), p.258; see also World Hunger Education Service Home Page Editorial, 'The US Contribution to IFAD [the International Fund for Agricultural Development]: A Day Late and a Dollar Short'. The United States is reducing its funding for IFAD – 'the only UN agency which devotes all of its resources to programmes which are targeted directly to strengthening the productivity of poor rural people' – by 66 per cent, a crippling blow. ([RTF bookmark start: _Hlt428168818][RTF bookmark end: _Hlt428168818] Articles/WFS/EDIT2.html)

27. See JimWhitman, 'Military Risk and Political Commitment in UN Humanitarian Peace Support Operations', in Eric Belgrad and Nitza Nachmias (eds), *The Politics of International Humanitarian Operations*, London: Praeger, 1997, pp.19–36.

28. See Mark Duffield, 'Complex Emergencies and the Crisis of Developmentalism', *IDS Bulletin*, Vol.25, No.4, 1994, pp.37–45.

29. Quoted in Gérard Prunier, *The Rwanda Crisis: History of a* Genocide, New York: Columbia University Press, 1995, p.302.

30. Paul Webster, 'Chirac "encouraged Kabila's foes"', *The Guardian*, 8 Aug. 1998.

31. Antonio Donini, 'Asserting Humanitarianism in Peace-Maintenance', *Global Governance*, Vol.4, No.1, Jan.–Mar. 1998, p.82.

32. Ibid, pp.82–96.

33. Thomas G. Weiss and Amir Pasic, 'Reinventing UNHCR: Enterprising Humanitarians in the Former Yugoslavia, 1991–1995', in *Global Governance*, Vol.3, No.1, Jan.–Apr., 1997, pp.41–57.

34. Statement of Mrs Sadako Ogata, UN High Commissioner for Refugees, at the Humanitarian Issues Working Group of the Peace Implementation Council, Geneva, 16 Dec. 1996.

35. Thomas G. Weiss and Larry Minear, *Humanitarianism Across Borders: Sustaining Civilians in Times of War*, London: Lynne Rienner Publishers., 1993.

36. Cedric Thornberry, 'Peacekeepers, Humanitarian Aid and Civil Conflicts', in Whitman and Pocock (eds.) (see N.24)., p.232.

37. International Federation of Red Cross and Red Crescent Societies, *World Disasters Report 1996*, Oxford: Oxford University Press, 1996, p.81.

38. Given extreme but nonetheless indicative expression by Laurent Kabila, President of the Democratic Republic of Congo, who denounced UNHCR as 'the sum total of all the conspiracies against our sovereignty'. Quoted in Mark Cutts, 'Prime Targets', *The World Today*, Aug./Sept. 1998, p.221.

39. UNICEF, *The State of the World's Children 1996*, Oxford: Oxford University Press.
40. Joel E. Oestreich, 'UNICEF and the Implementation of the Convention on the Rights of the Child', *Global Governance* 4 (1998), pp.184–5.
41. See Jeremy Ginifer, *Beyond the Emergency: Development Within UN Peace Missions*, London and Portland, OR: Frank Cass, 1997.
42. UN DHA Integrated Regional Information Network, 7 Jan. 1997.
43. Michael Platzer, 'Temporary Protection of a Persecuted People', in David Wippman (ed.), *International Law and Ethnic Conflict*, Ithaca: Cornell University Press, 1998, p.239.
44. Maragaret Joan Anstee, *Orphan of the Cold War: The Inside Story of the Collapse of the Angolan Peace Process, 1992–3*, London: Macmillan, 1996, p.39 (italics original).
45. For a detailed statistical breakdown, see The Financial Tracking Database for Complex Emergencies at http://www.reliefweb.int/fts/index.html
46. Shepard Forman and Rita Parhad, 'Paying for Essentials: Resources for Humanitarian Assistance', New York: Center on International Cooperation (paper prepared for meeting at Pocantico Conference Center of the Rockerfeller Brothers Fund), reprinted in the *Journal of Humanitarian Assistance*. http://www–jha.sps.cam.ac.uk.
47. Hannah Arendt, *The Human Condition*, Chicago: The University of Chicago Press, 1958, p.220.
48. Antonio Donini, 'Asserting Humanitarianism in Peace-Maintenance' (see N.31), p.84.
49. James C. Ingram, 'The Future Architecture for International Humanitarian Assistance', in Weiss and Minear (see N.35), pp.171–93.

Notes on Contributors

Yves Beigbeder holds a doctorate in Public Law. A former WHO official, he is now an Adjunct Professor at Webster University, Geneva. He lectures on international organization and administration there and for UNITAR as a Senior Fellow. He has written several books and articles on UN organizations and their management, including WHO.

Dennis Dijkzeul earned his PhD on the management of multilateral organizations at the Rotterdam School of Management in the Netherlands. Recently, he has been working as an independent consultant for UNOPS in New York and Geneva, and The War-torn Societies Project (Geneva: UNRISD/PSIS). His main interest is the management of organizations active in rebuilding societies devastated by war.

Leon Gordenker is Professor Emeritus of Politics and Research Associate of the Center of International Studies at Princeton University. He is also a research fellow at the Ralph Bunche Institute on the United Nations at City University of New York. He is the editor of *The Challenging Role of the UN Secretary-General* (with Benjamin Rivlin) and author of *The United Nations in the 1990s* (with Peter R. Baehr).

Raymond F. Hopkins is Richter Professor of Political Science at Swarthmore College, Pennsylvania. He has published widely on food policy, public policy, international and African politics and has acted as a consultant to the World Food Programme, the Food and Agriculture Organization, the World Bank and USAID.

Deborah Waller Meyers is an Associate in the International Migration Policy Program at the Carnegie Endowment for International Peace. She works on the international refugee regime, the US immigration system, and the US–Mexico relationship. She served as a policy analyst at the US Commission on Immigration Reform and as a consultant for RAND and the Inter-American Dialogue. She earned her MA in International Affairs from George Washington University and her BA from Brandeis University.

Kathleen Newland is a Senior Associate in the International Migration Policy Program at the Carnegie Endowment for International Peace, which she joined in 1994. Her work focuses on refugee policy and international humanitarian response. She also co-directs the Migration and Citizenship project in the Carnegie Moscow Center. Immediately before joining the

Endowment, she was an independent consultant, with the UN High Commissioner for Refugees, the World Bank and the Office of the UN Secretary-General as her principal clients. In 1992–93, she wrote the first *State of the World's Refugees* for UNHCR. From 1988 to 1992, she lectured at the London School of Economics, becoming a full-time member of the International Relations Faculty in 1990.

Thomas G. Weiss is Distinguished Professor of Political Science at The Graduate School and University Center of The City University of New York. From 1990 to 1998 as a Research Professor at Brown University's Thomas J. Watson Jr. Institute for International Studies, he also held a number of administrative assignments (Director of the Global Security Program, Associate Dean of the Faculty, Associate Director), served as the Executive Director of the Academic Council on the UN System, and codirected the Humanitarianism and War Project. His latest book is *Military–Civilian Interactions: Intervening in Humanitarian Crises* (1999).

Jim Whitman is a member of the Faculty of Social and Political Sciences, Cambridge University. He is the co-editor of the *Journal of Humanitarian Assistance* and general editor of the forthcoming Macmillan series, *Global Issues*.

Index